First Printing: 2020

ISBN 978-0-244-24875-8

Corn Grenouille Muldoon
De Constant Rebecqueplein 20b. Atelier 3.03
2518RA, The Hague, The Netherlands
secornelisse@gmail.com
www.seancornelisse.com

Ordering Information:
Special discounts are available on quantity purchases by corporations, associations, educators, and others. Also for enquiries about the original drawings. For details, contact the publisher at the above listed address.

ASEMIC CONNOTATIONS AND ASIA IN A BARBARIAN

SEANCORNELISSE

to Oskar

Sean Cornelisse (The Hague, Netherlands) is an artist who works in a variety of media. By experimenting with aleatoric processes, Cornelisse often creates work using creative game tactics, but these are never permissive. Play is a serious matter: during the game, different rules apply than in everyday life and even everyday objects undergo transubstantiation.

His artworks are characterized by the use of everyday objects in an atmosphere of middleclass mentality in which recognition plays an important role. By taking daily life as subject matter while commenting on the everyday aesthetic of middle class values, he formalizes the coincidental and emphasizes the conscious process of composition that is behind the seemingly random works. The thought processes, which are supposedly private, highly subjective and unfiltered in their references to dream worlds, are frequently revealed as assemblages.

His works demonstrate how life extends beyond its own subjective limits and often tells a story about the effects of global cultural interaction over the latter half of the twentieth century. It challenges the binaries we continually reconstruct between Self and Other, between our own 'cannibal' and 'civilized' selves. By applying a poetic and often metaphorical language, he wants to amplify the astonishment of the spectator by creating compositions or settings that generate tranquil poetic images that leave traces and balances on the edge of recognition and alienation.

His works appear as dreamlike images in which fiction and reality meet, well-known tropes merge, meanings shift, past and present fuse. Time and memory always play a key role. By investigating language on a meta-level, he tries to grasp language. Transformed into art, language becomes an ornament. At that moment, lots of ambiguities and indistinctnesses, which are inherent to the phenomenon, come to the surface.

His works feature coincidental, accidental and unexpected connections which make it possible to revise art history and, even better, to complement it. Combining unrelated aspects lead to surprising analogies. By demonstrating the omnipresent lingering of a 'corporate world', his works references post-colonial theory as well as the avant-garde or the post-modern and the left-wing democratic movement as a form of resistance against the logic of the capitalist market system.

His works focus on the inability of communication which is used to visualize reality, the attempt of dialogue, the dissonance between form and content and the dysfunctions of language. In short, the lack(?) of clear references are key elements in the work.[1]

---

[1] ArtyFartyBollocksGenerator.com

DA VINCI PETIT GRIS PUR 407/500 01945? Serie 418 GERMANY

In recent history, numerous articles and/or artist publications and initiatives have been written on the topic of 'asemic writing'. This to give   (reviewed) definitions or either it merely being a bundled manifestation of found aesthetics that he or she categorizes by asemic writing as such. So here is another one.

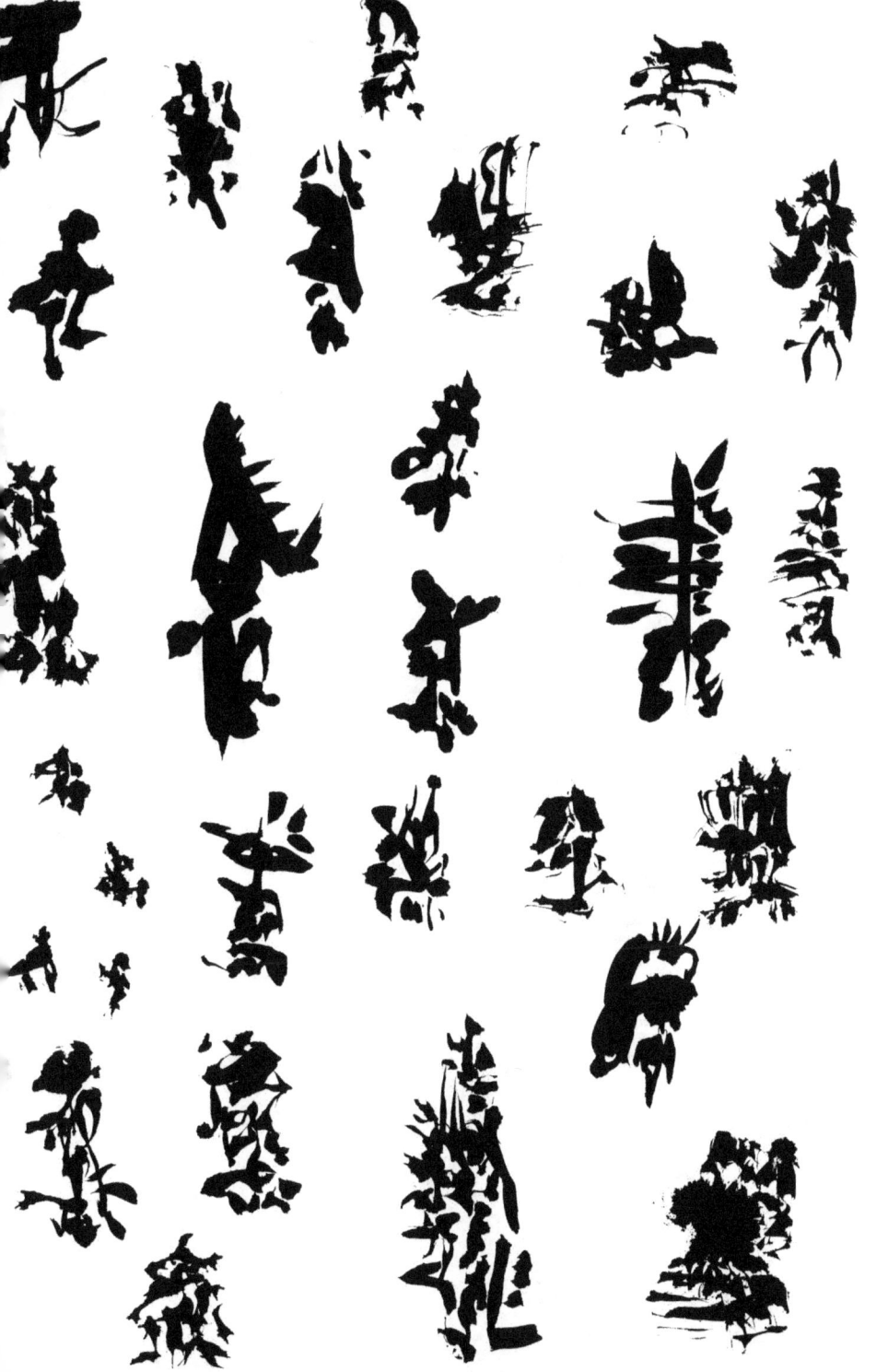

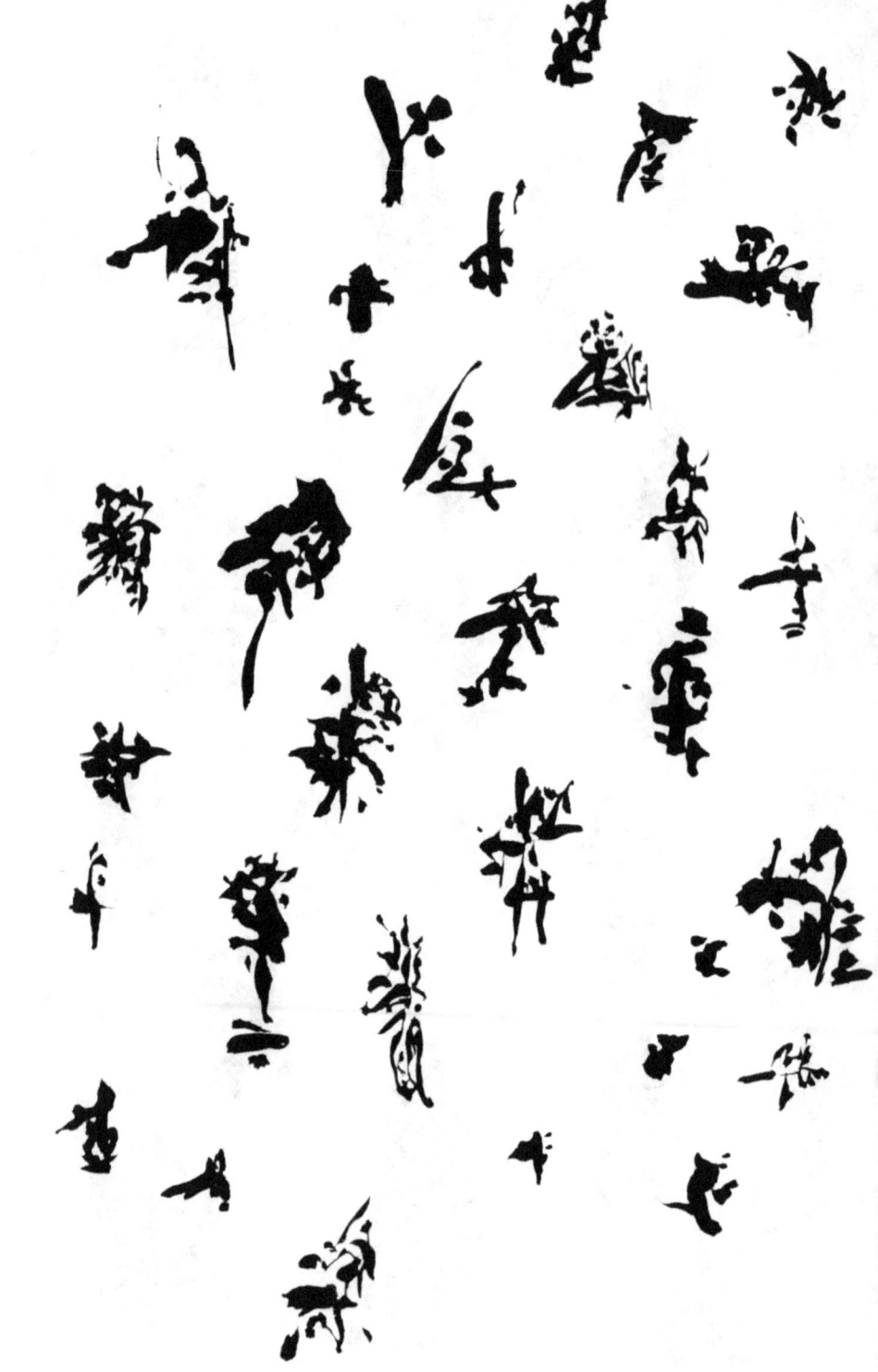

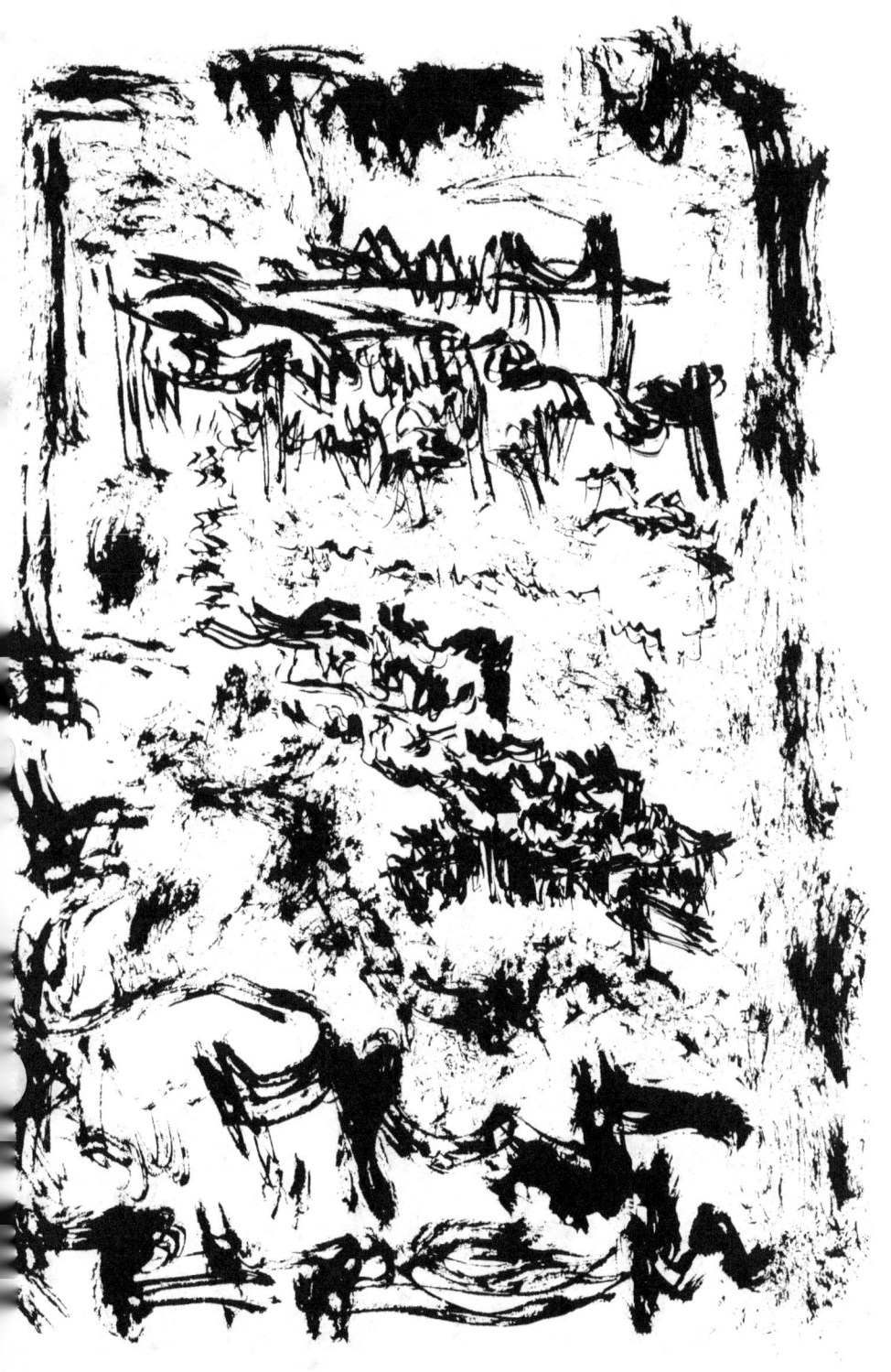

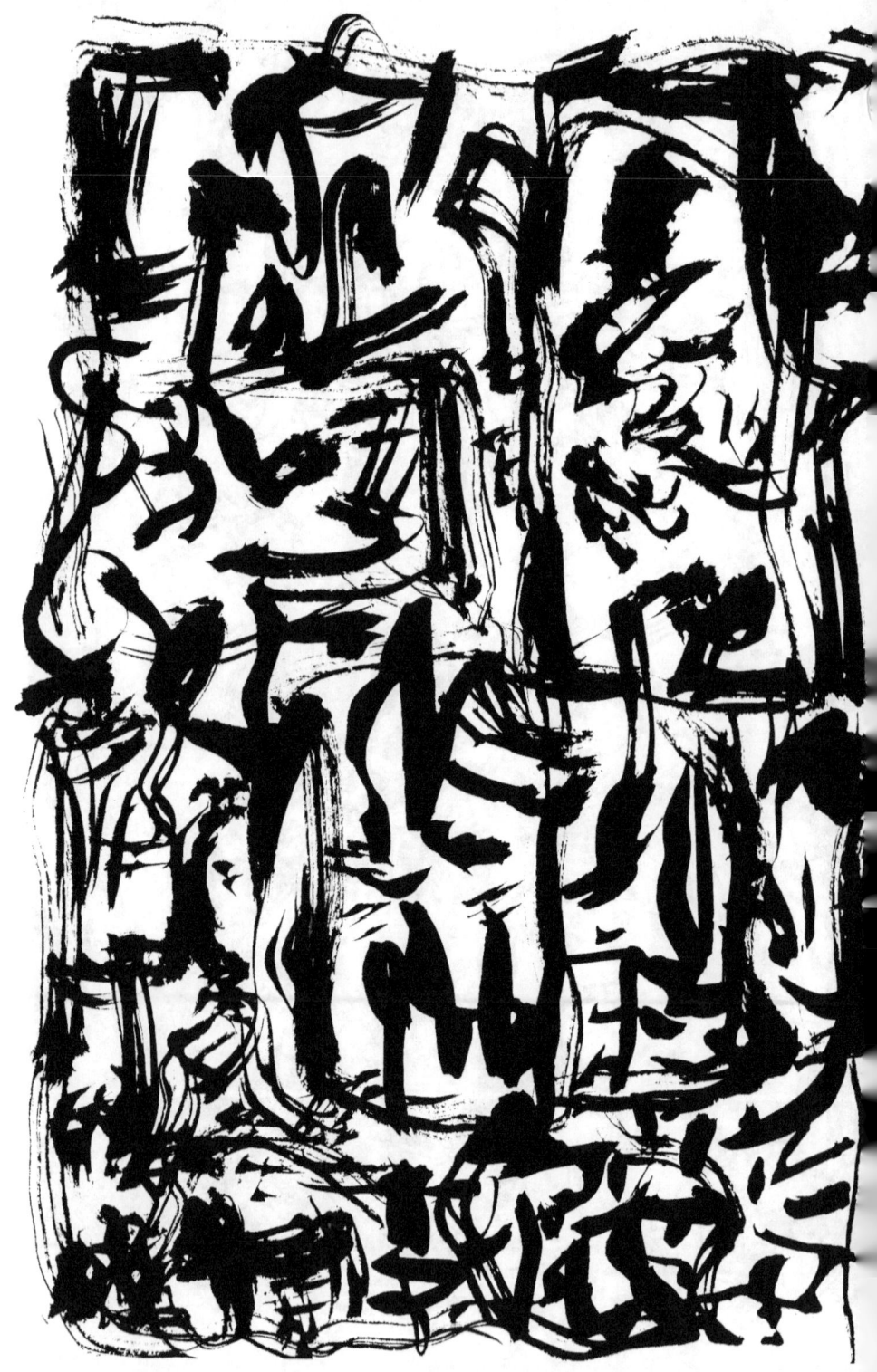

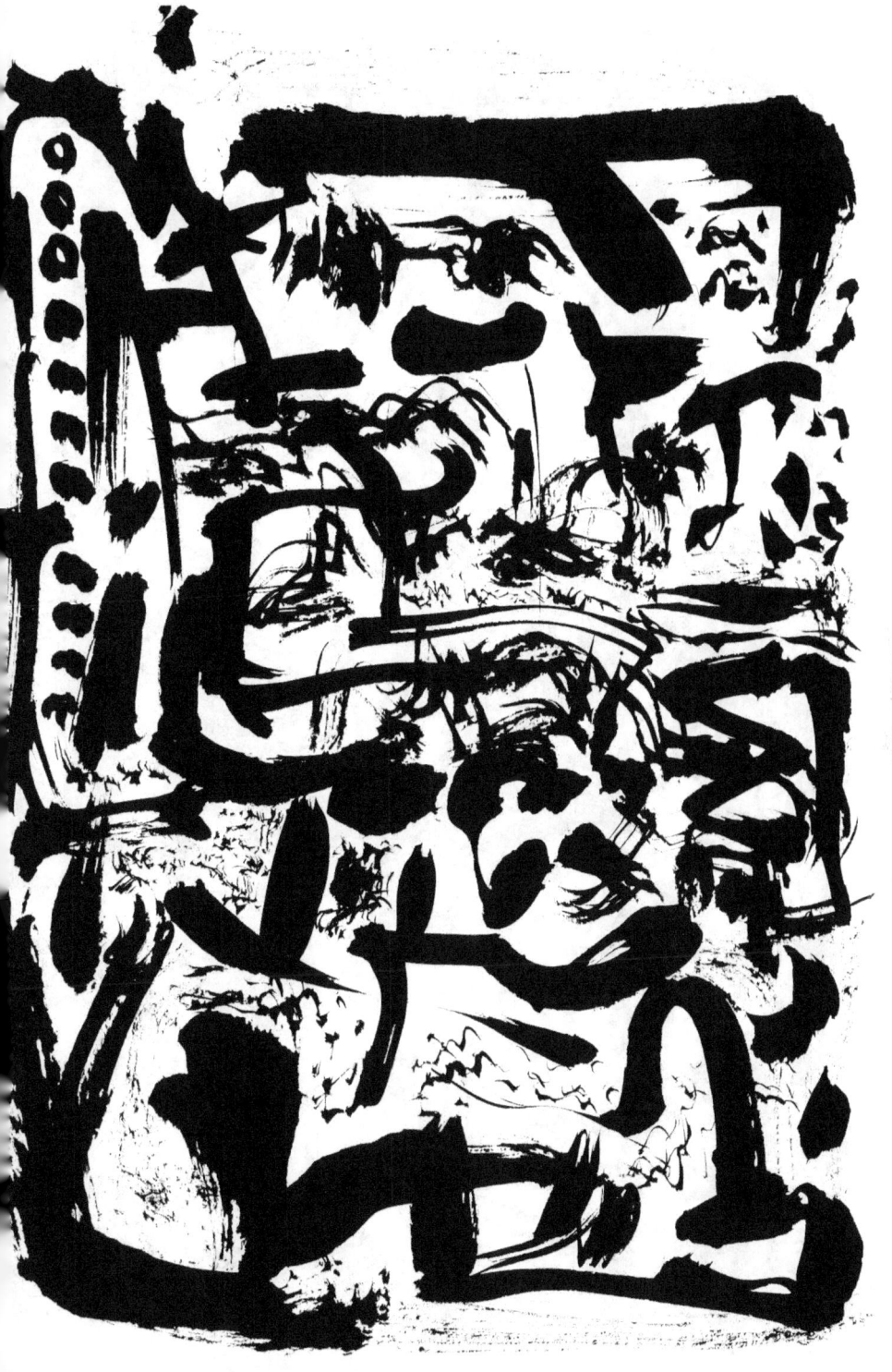

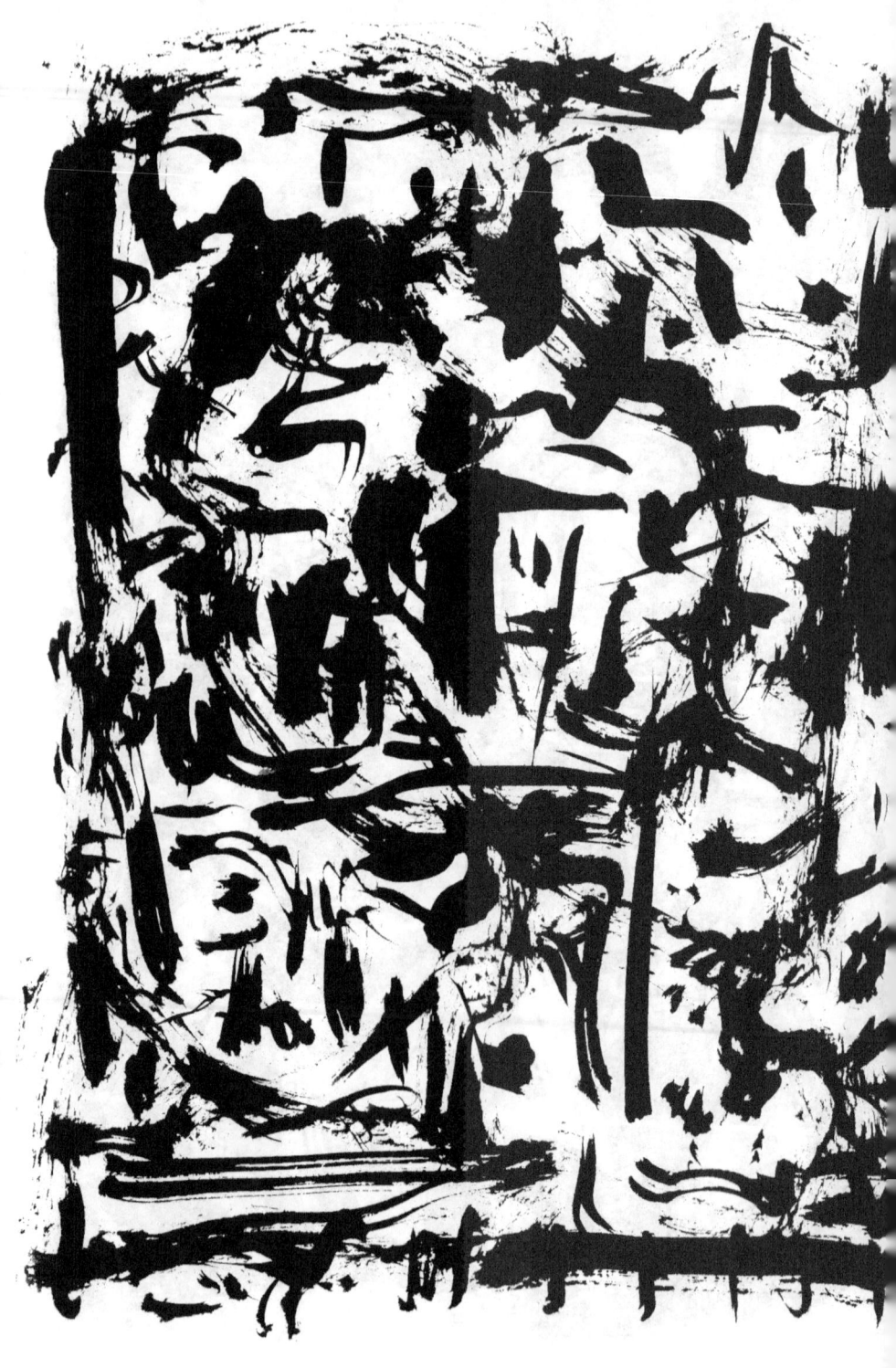

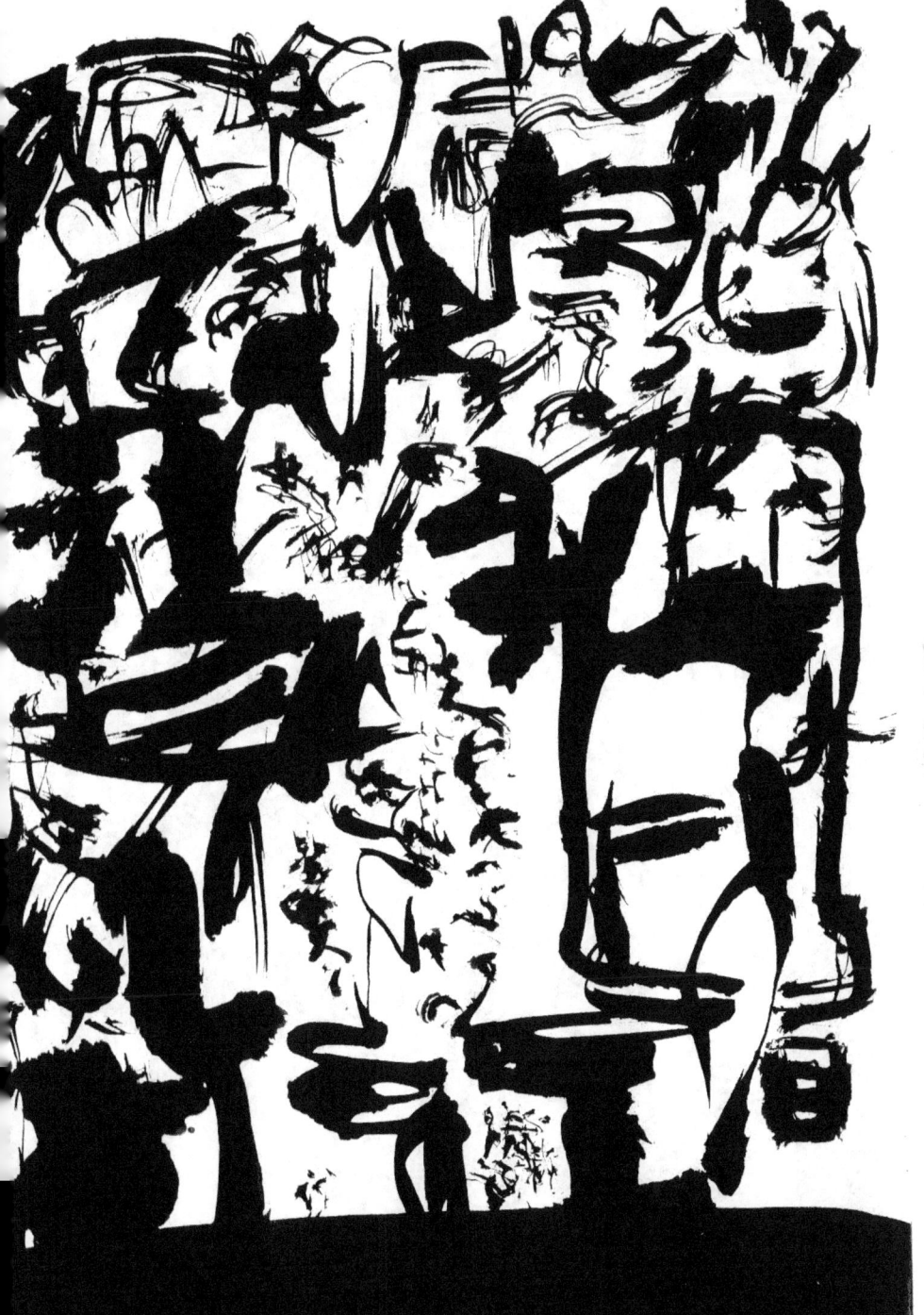

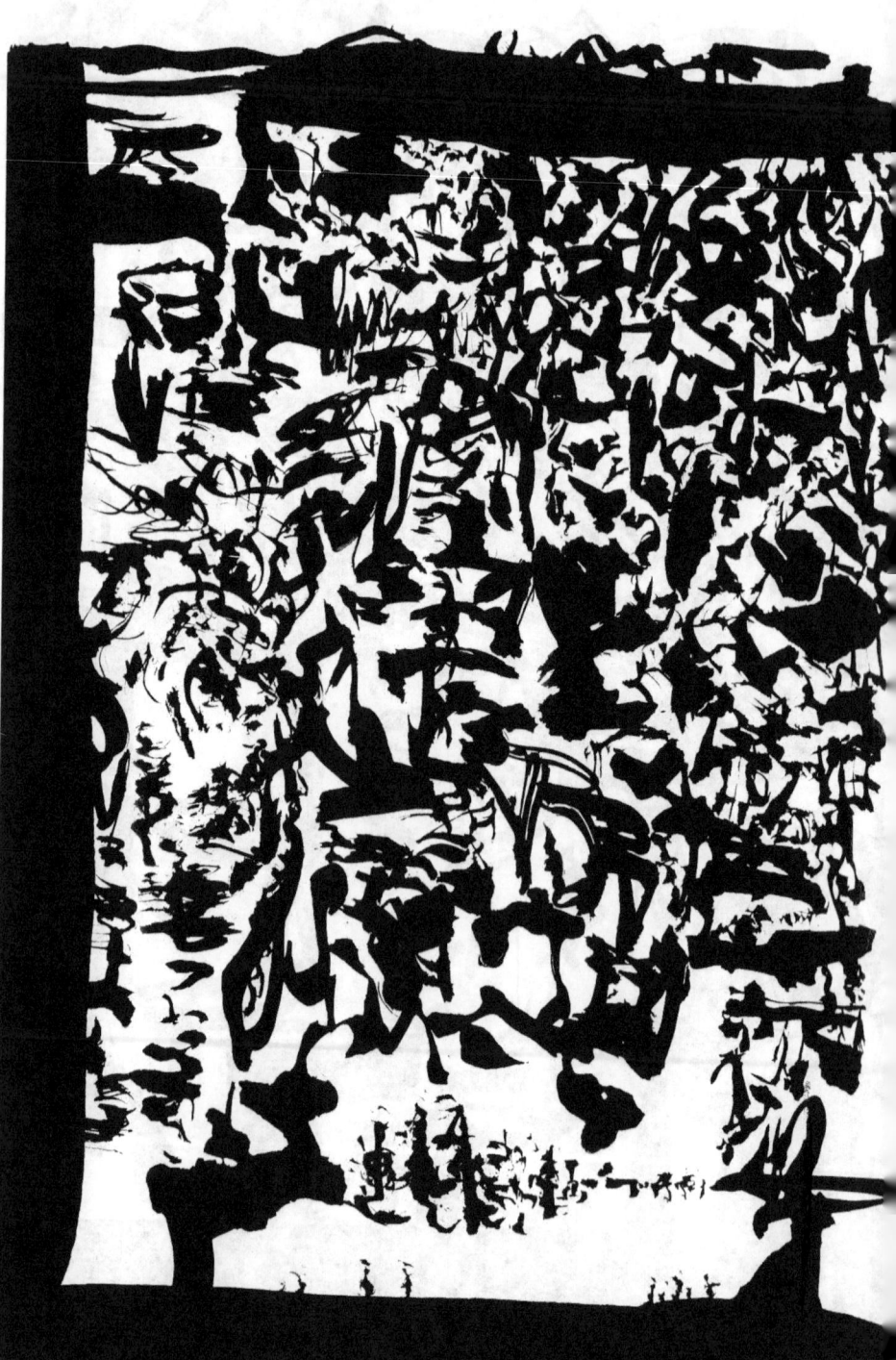

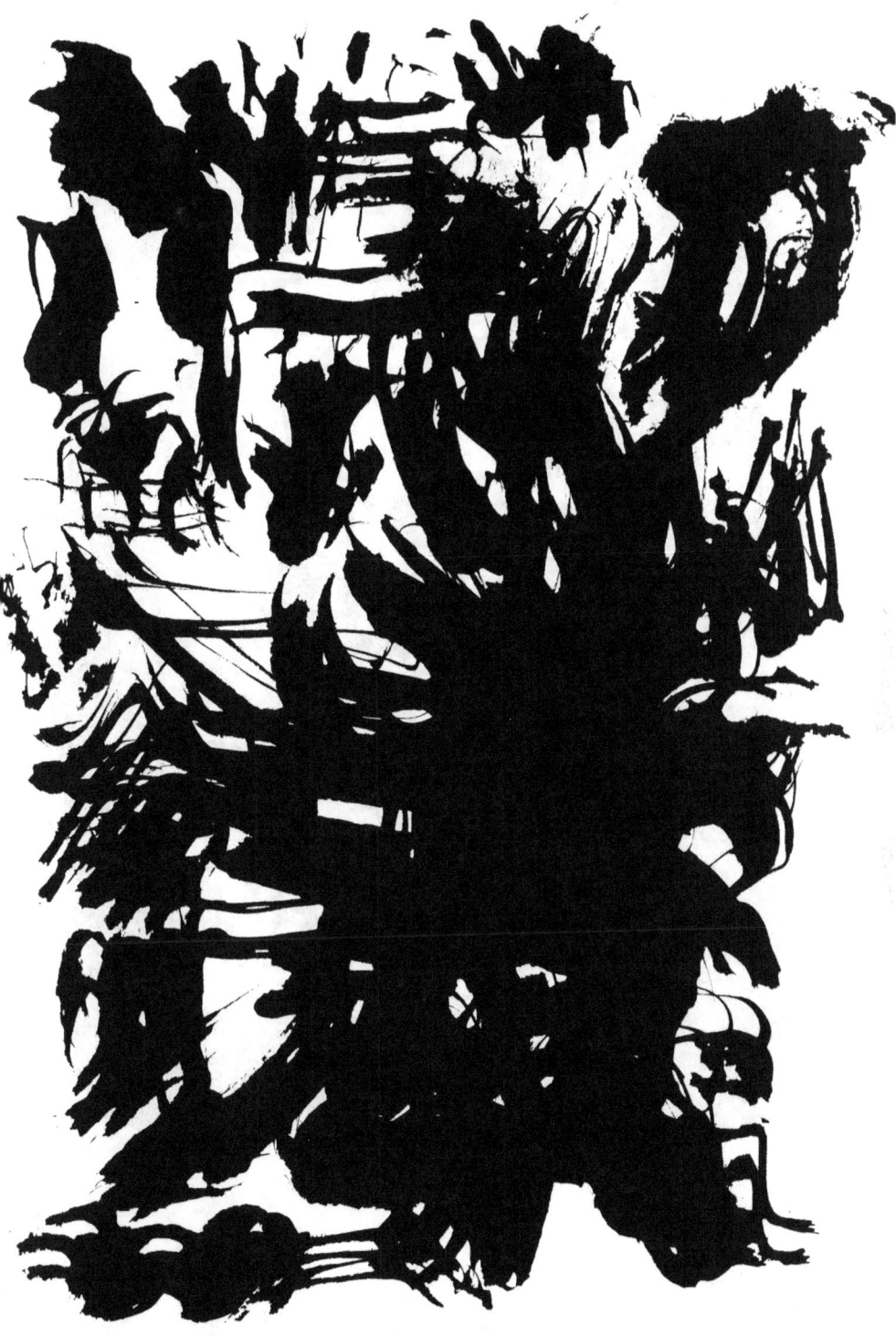

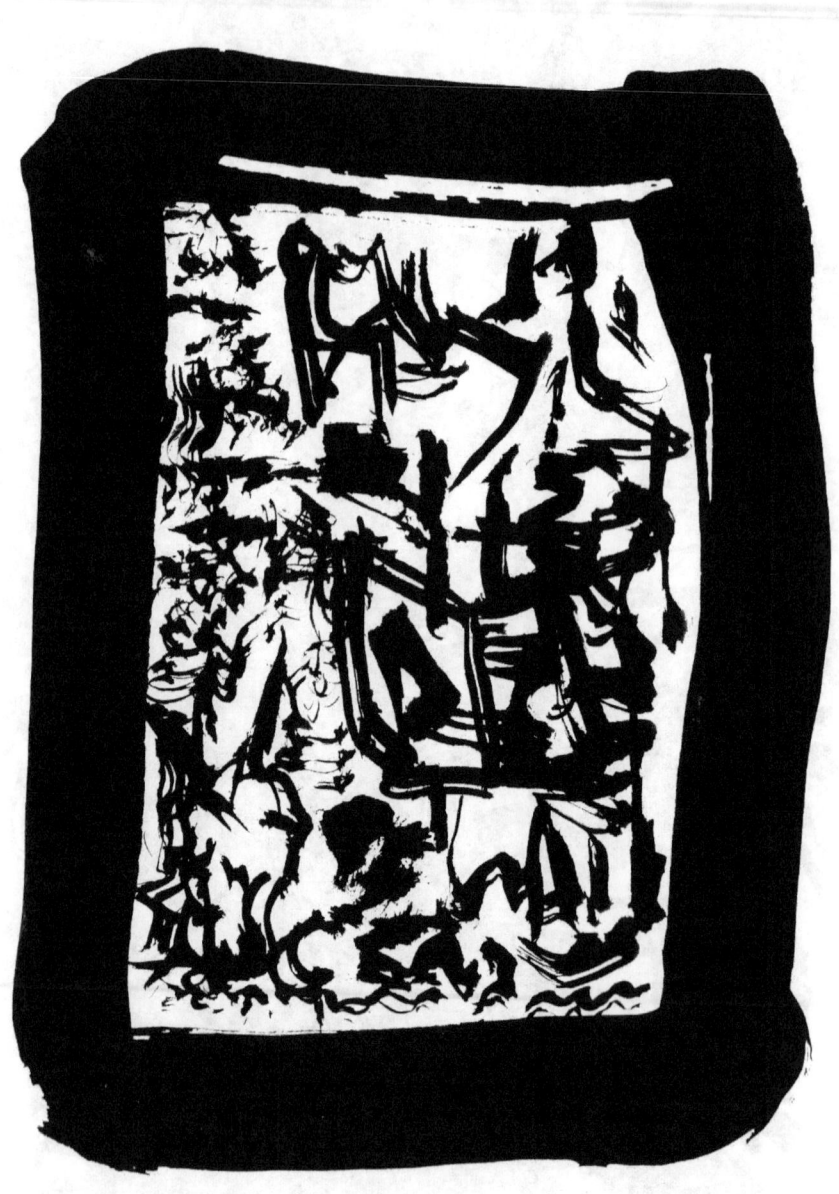

57 works, ink on A5 paper, made between November 2019 and January 2020.

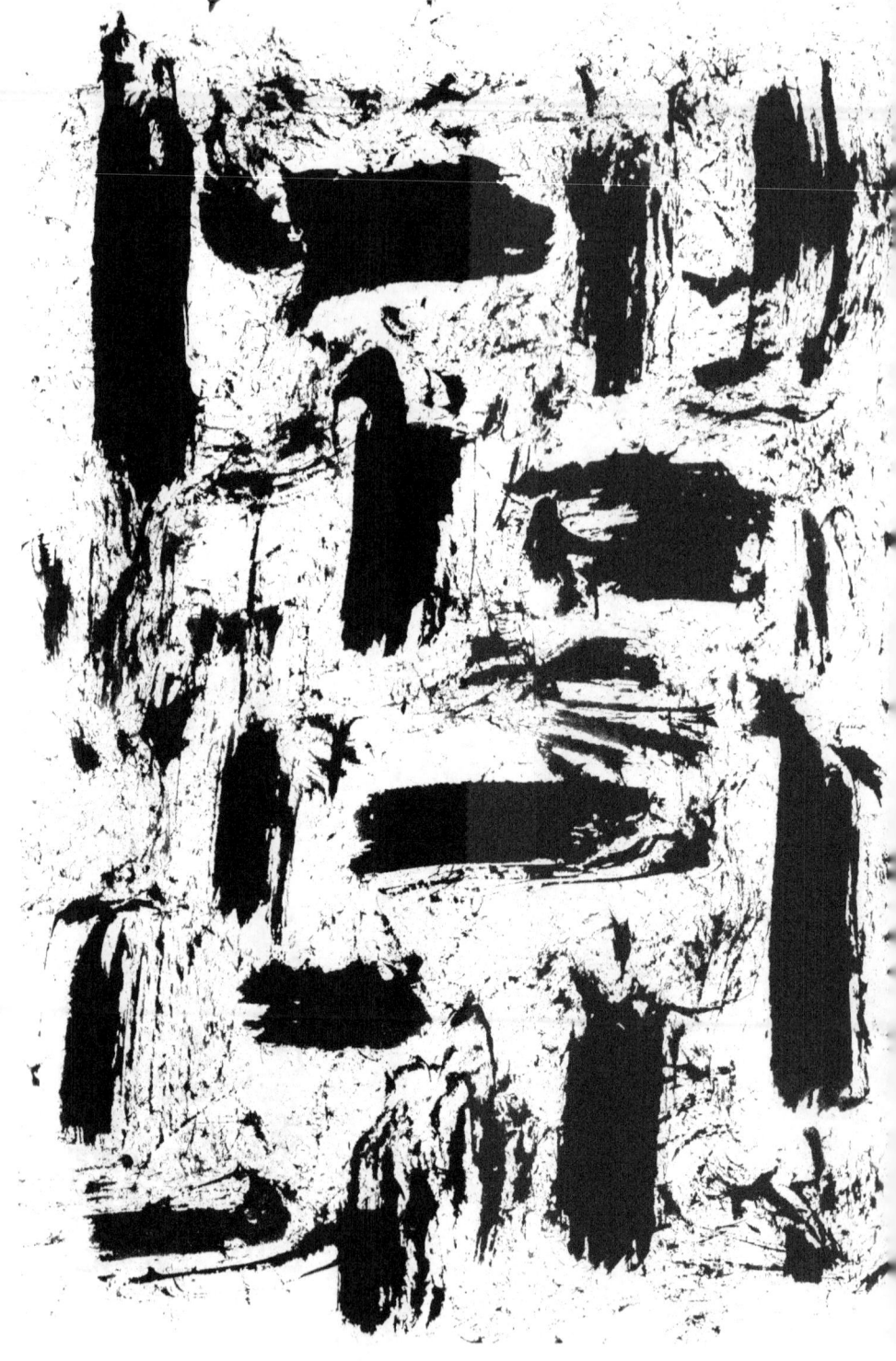

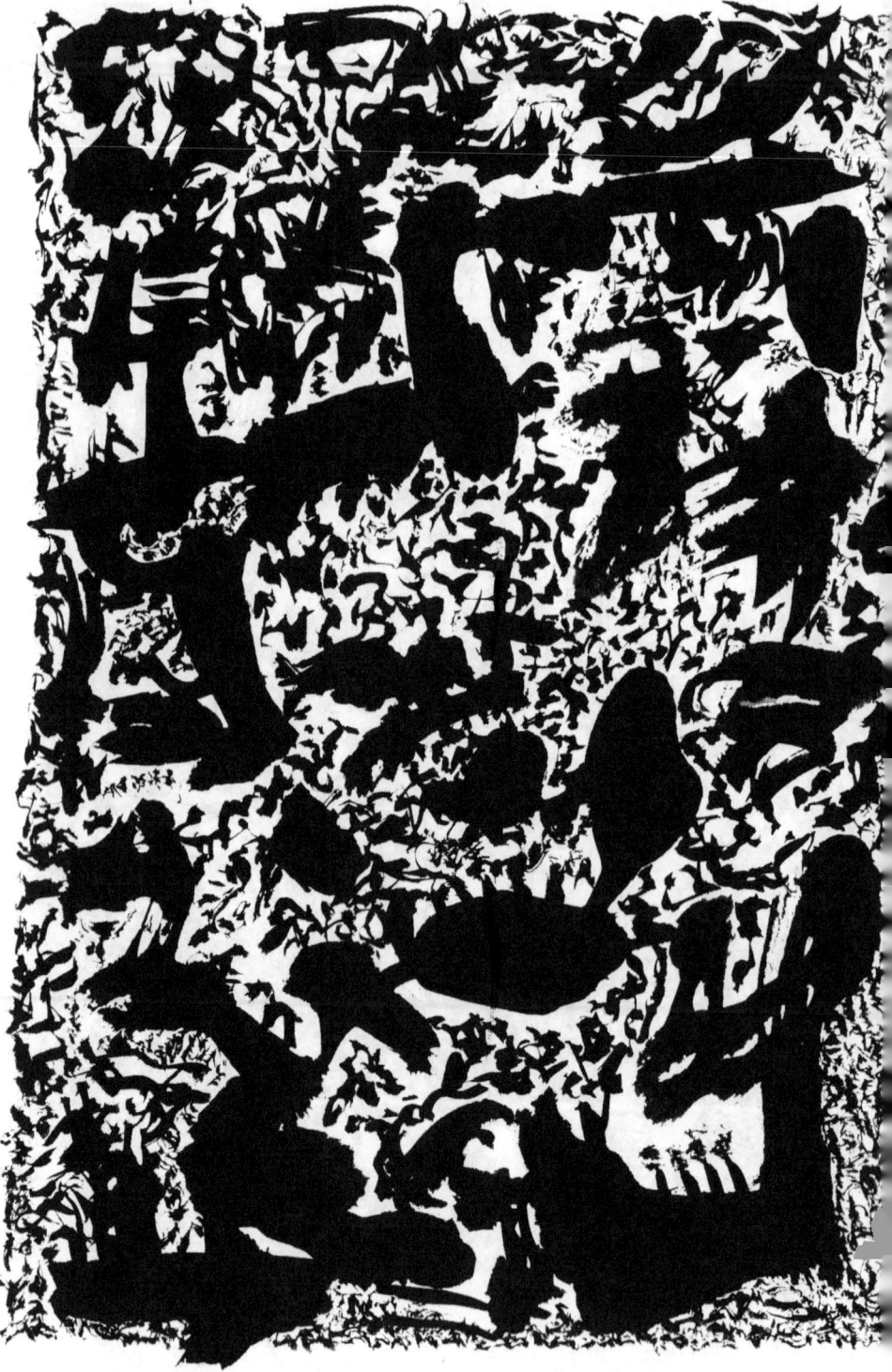

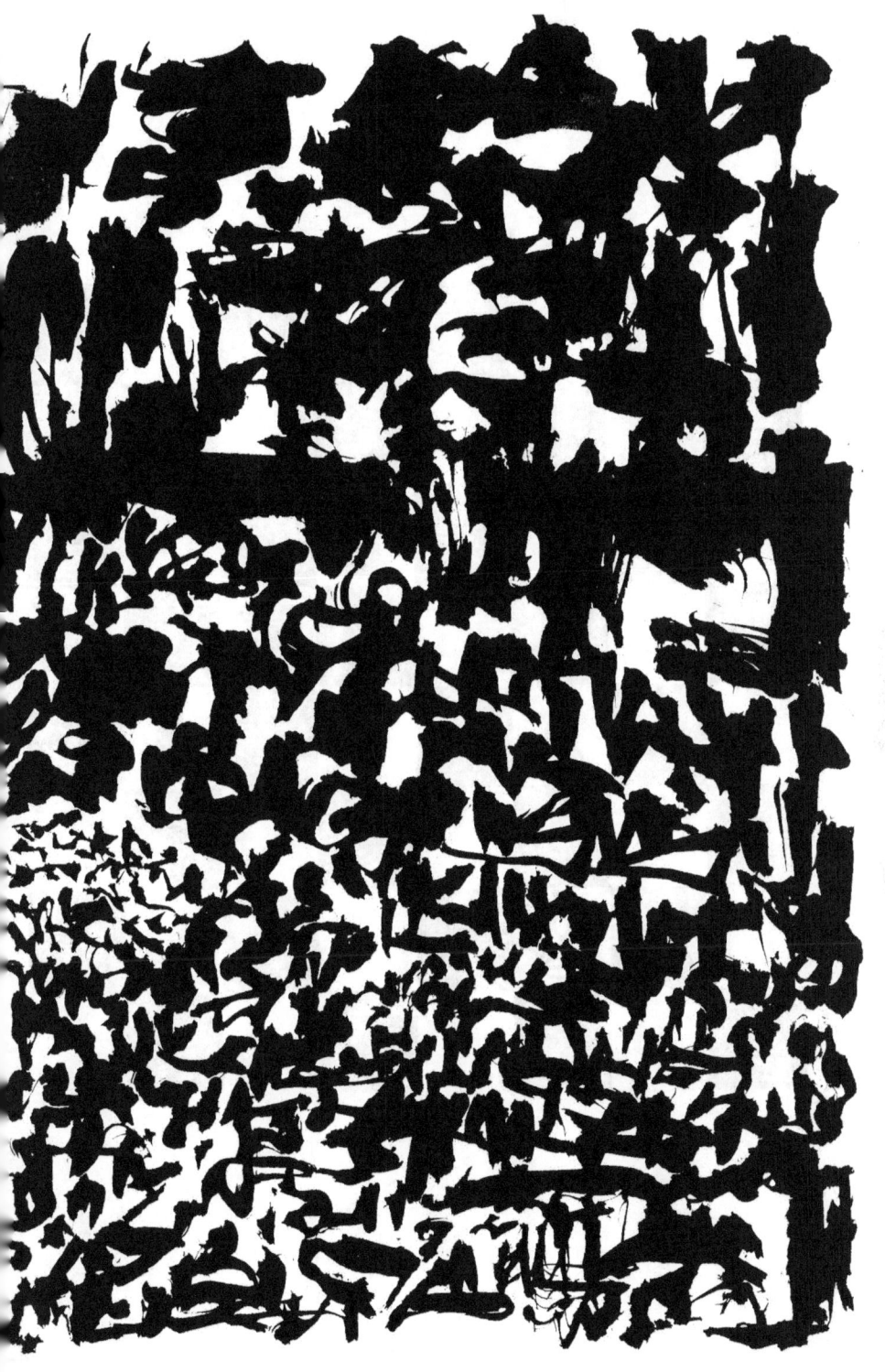

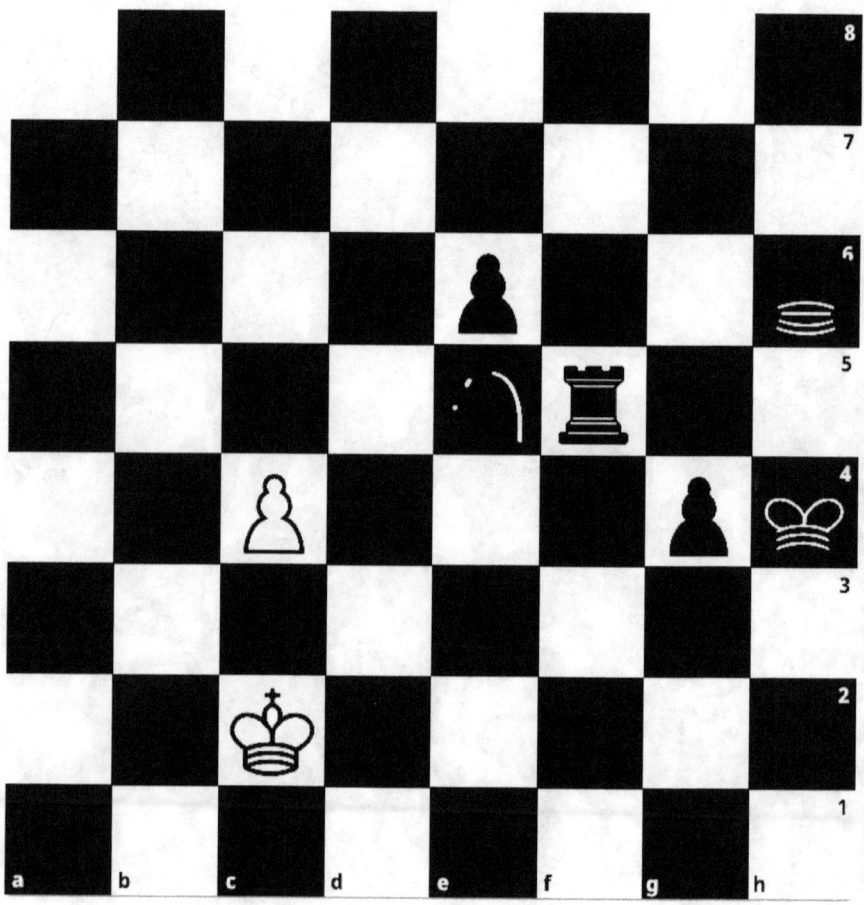

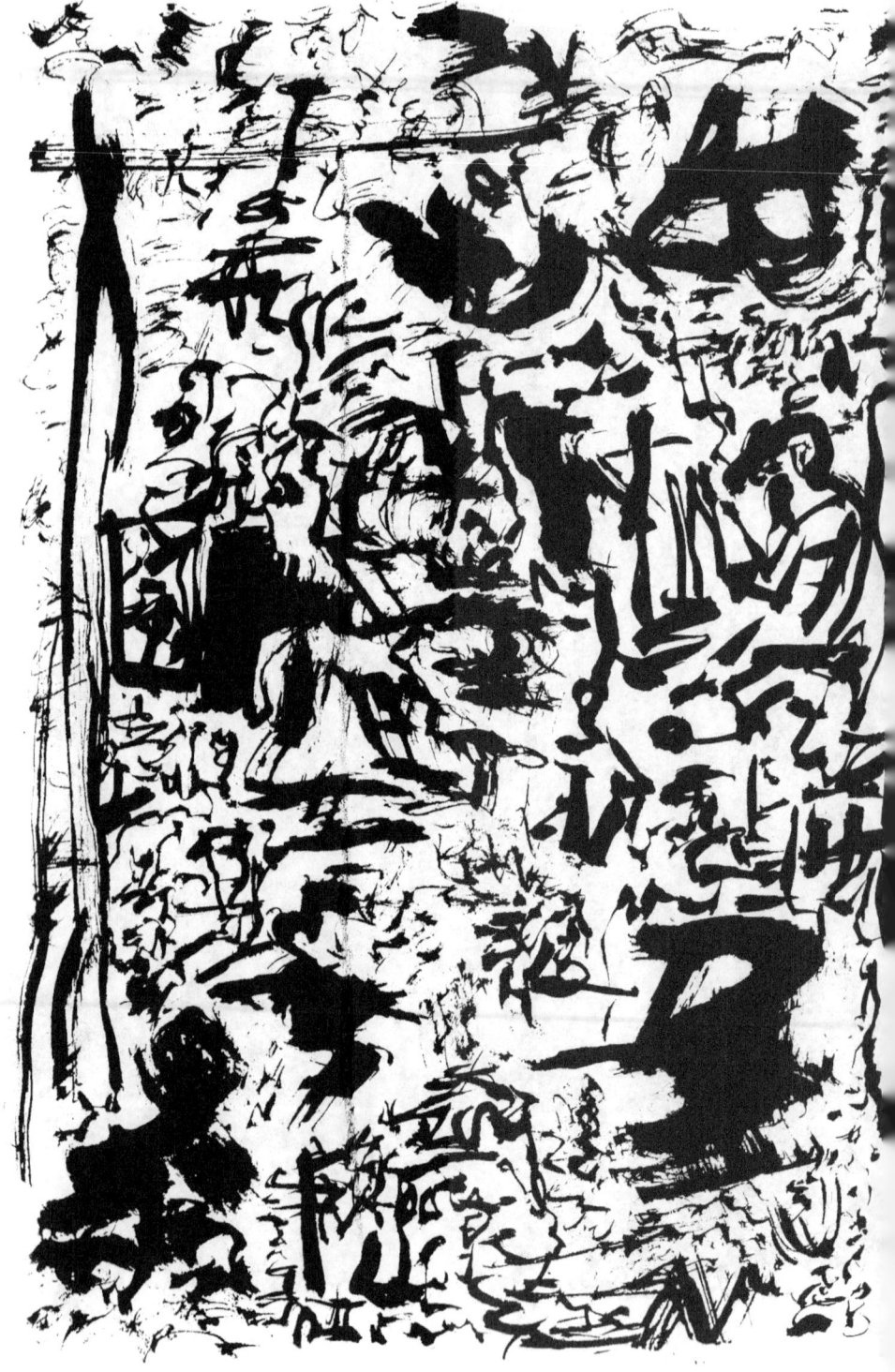

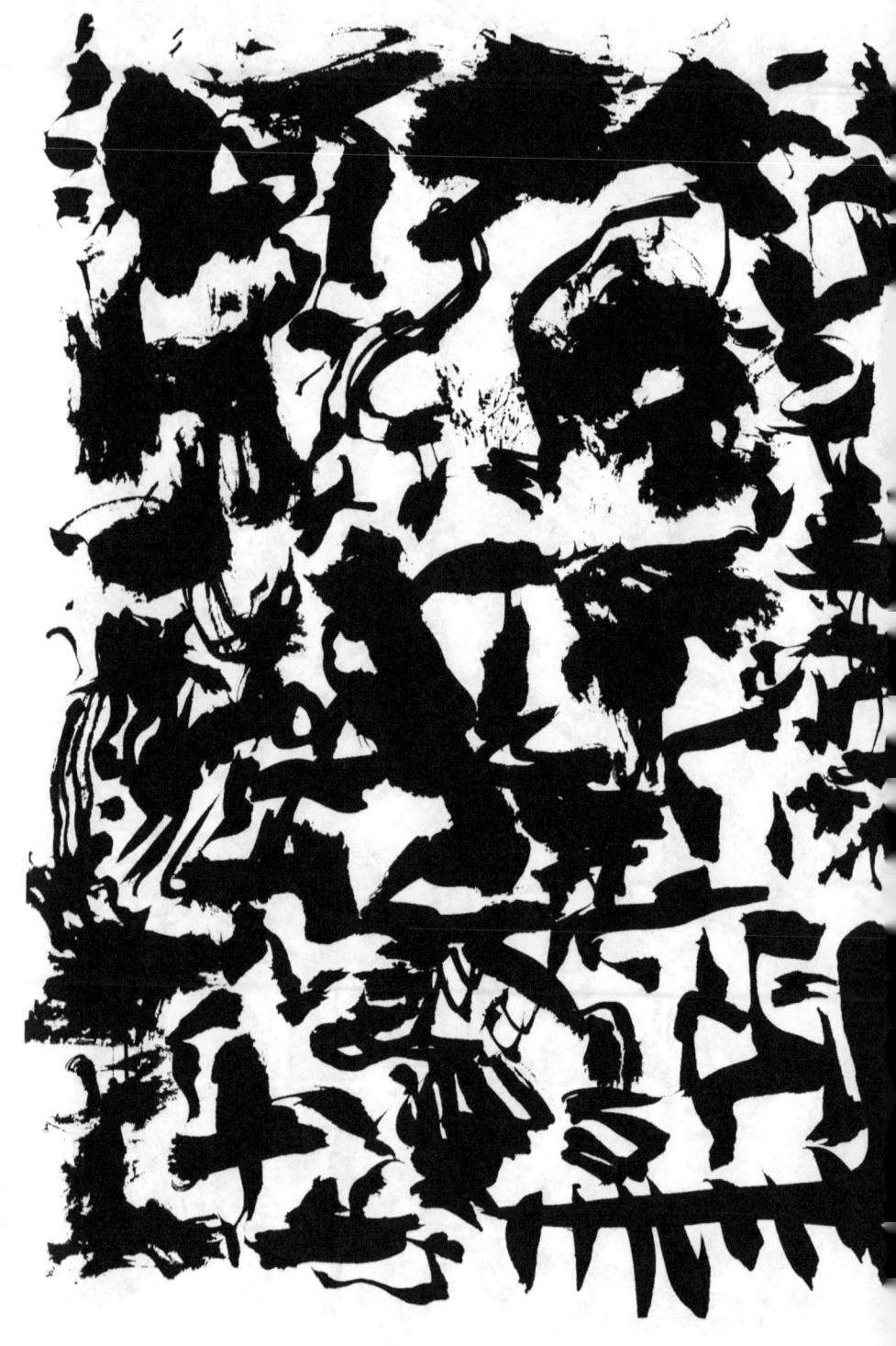

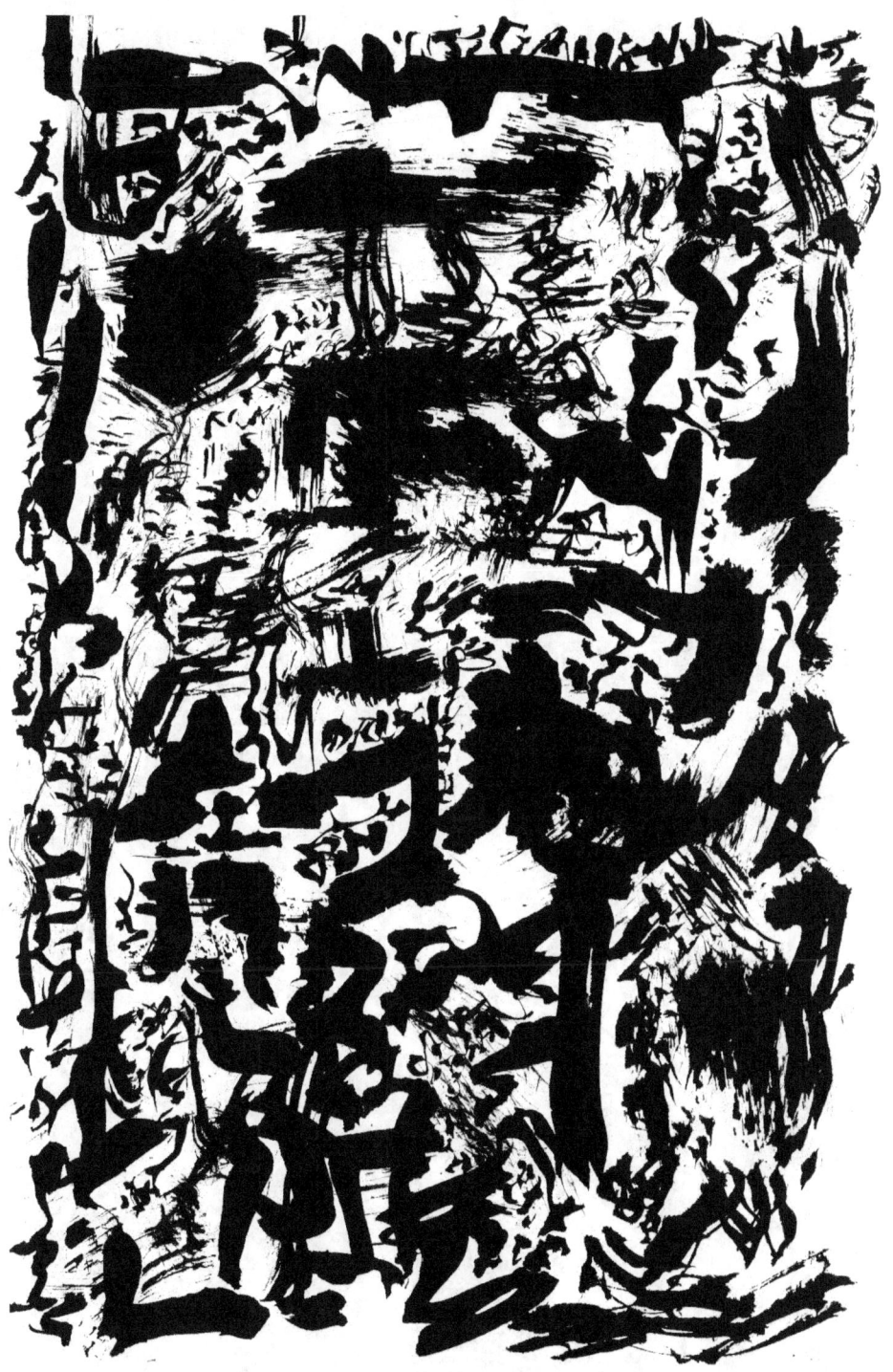

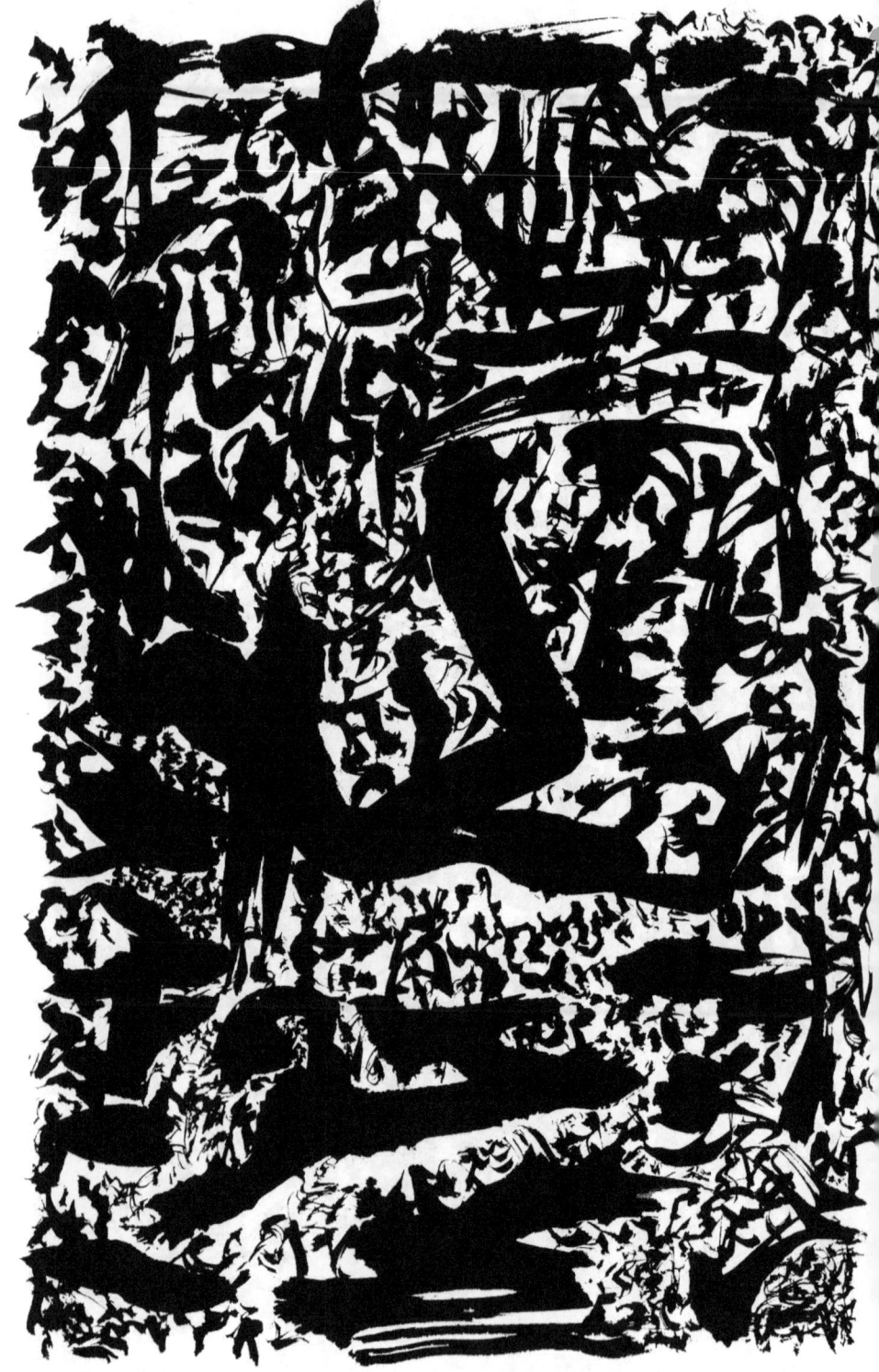

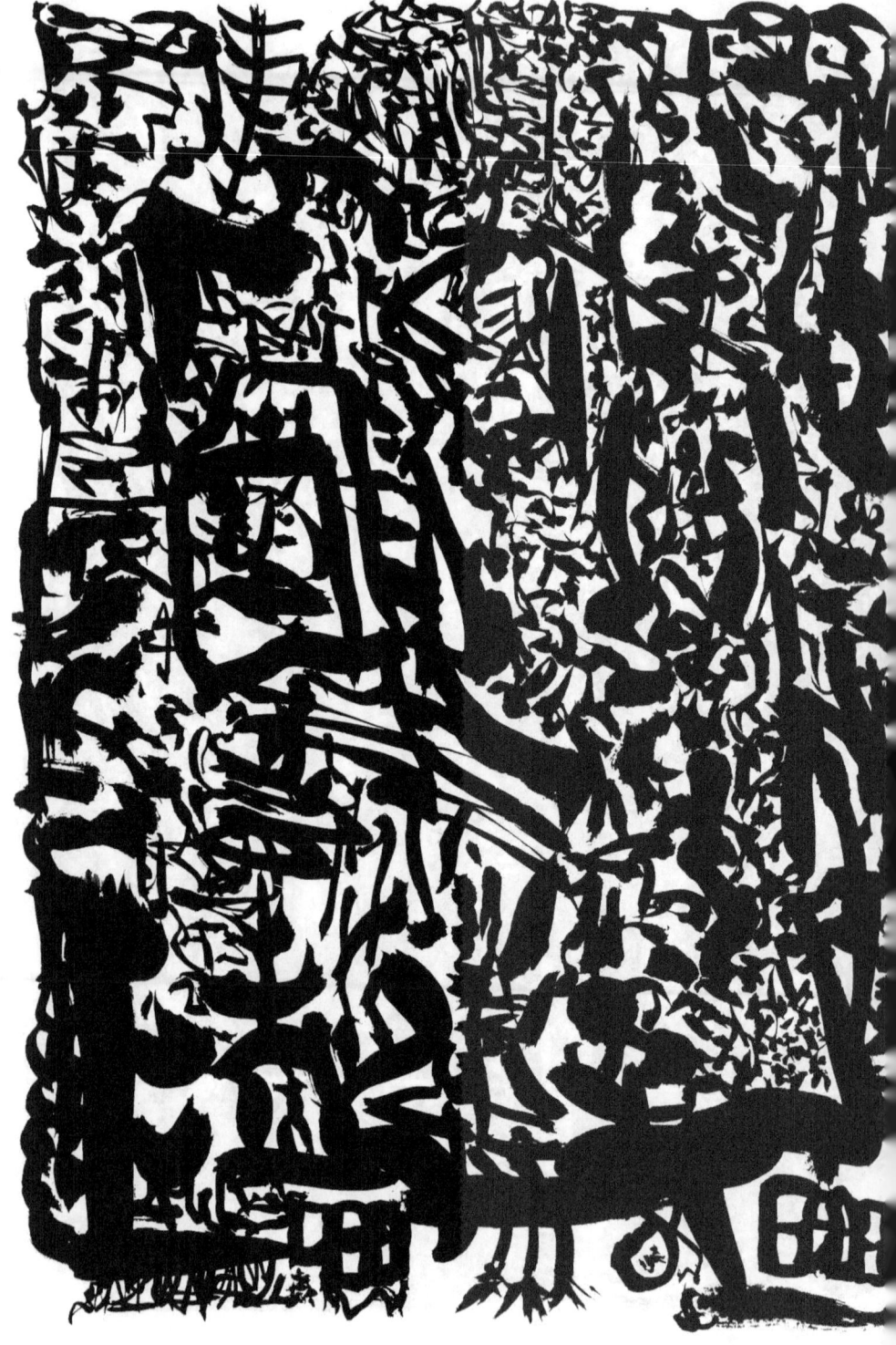

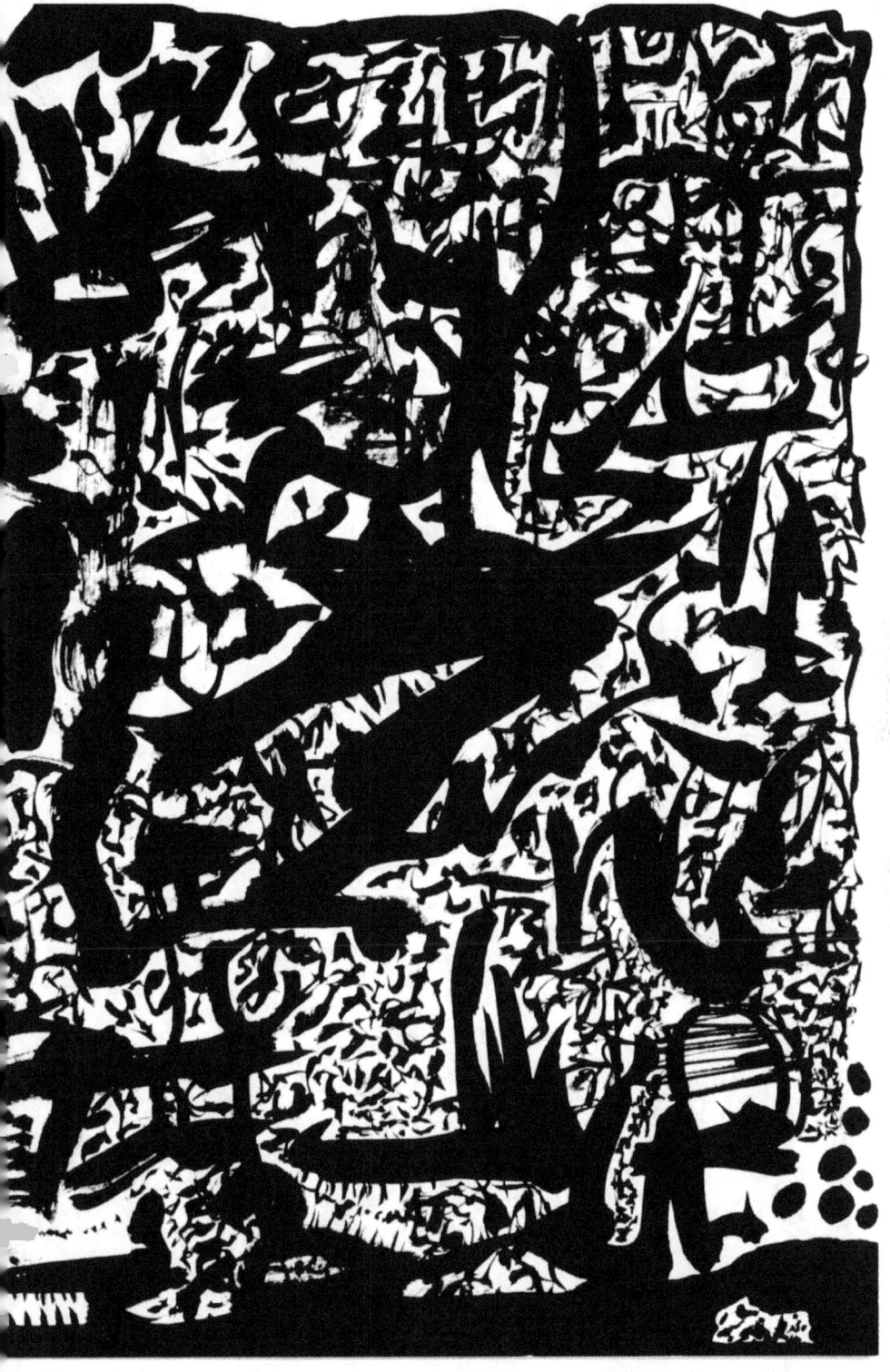

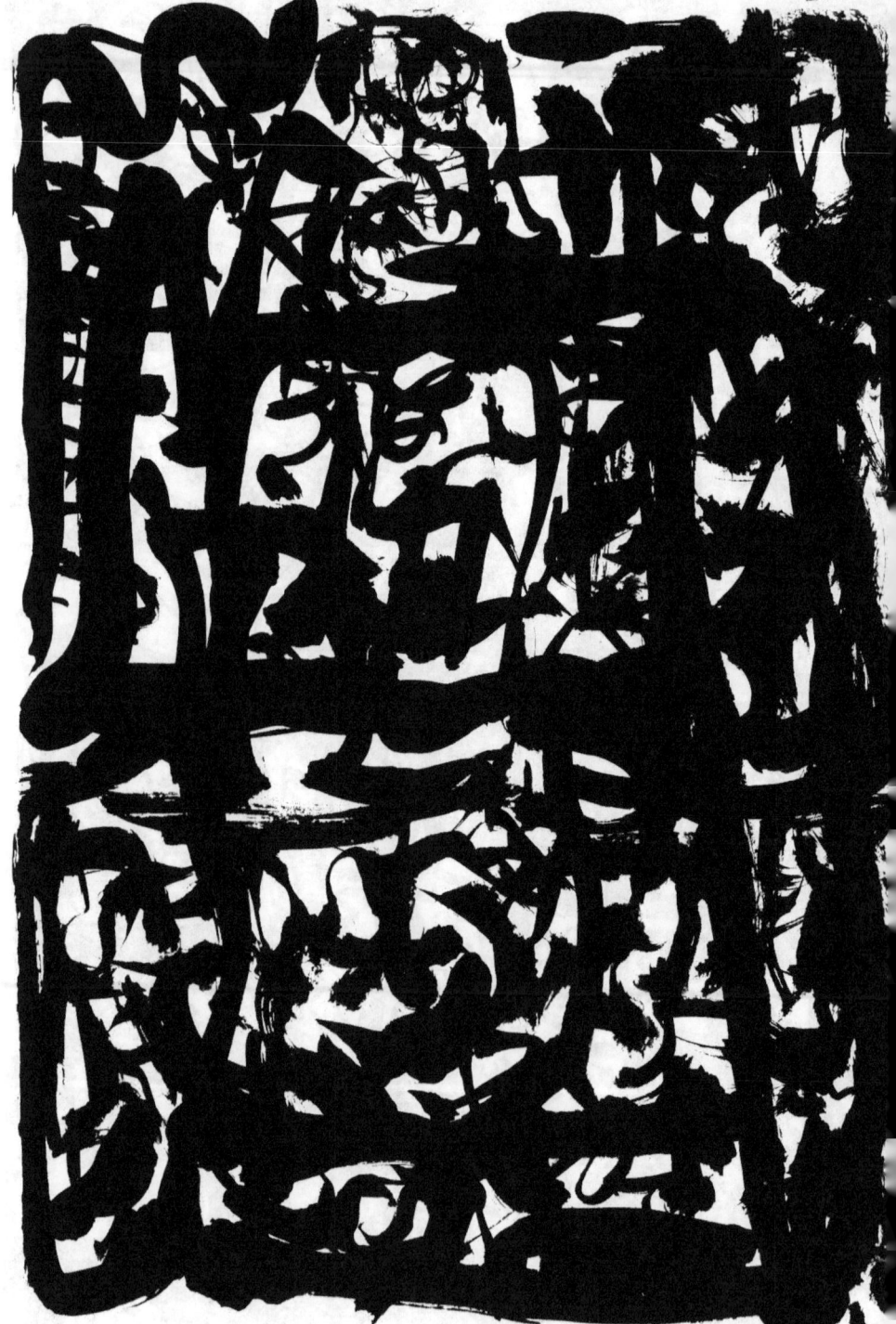

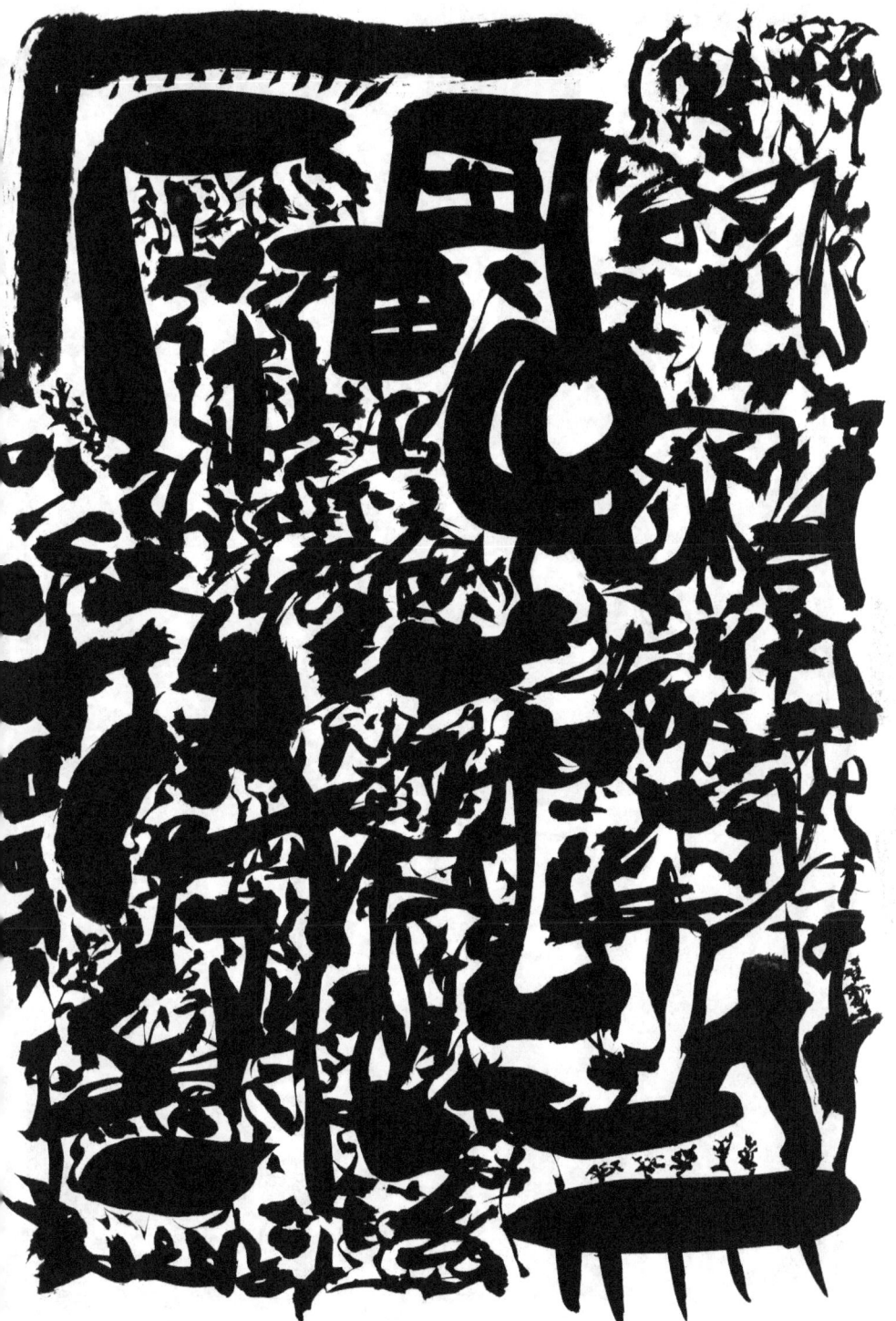

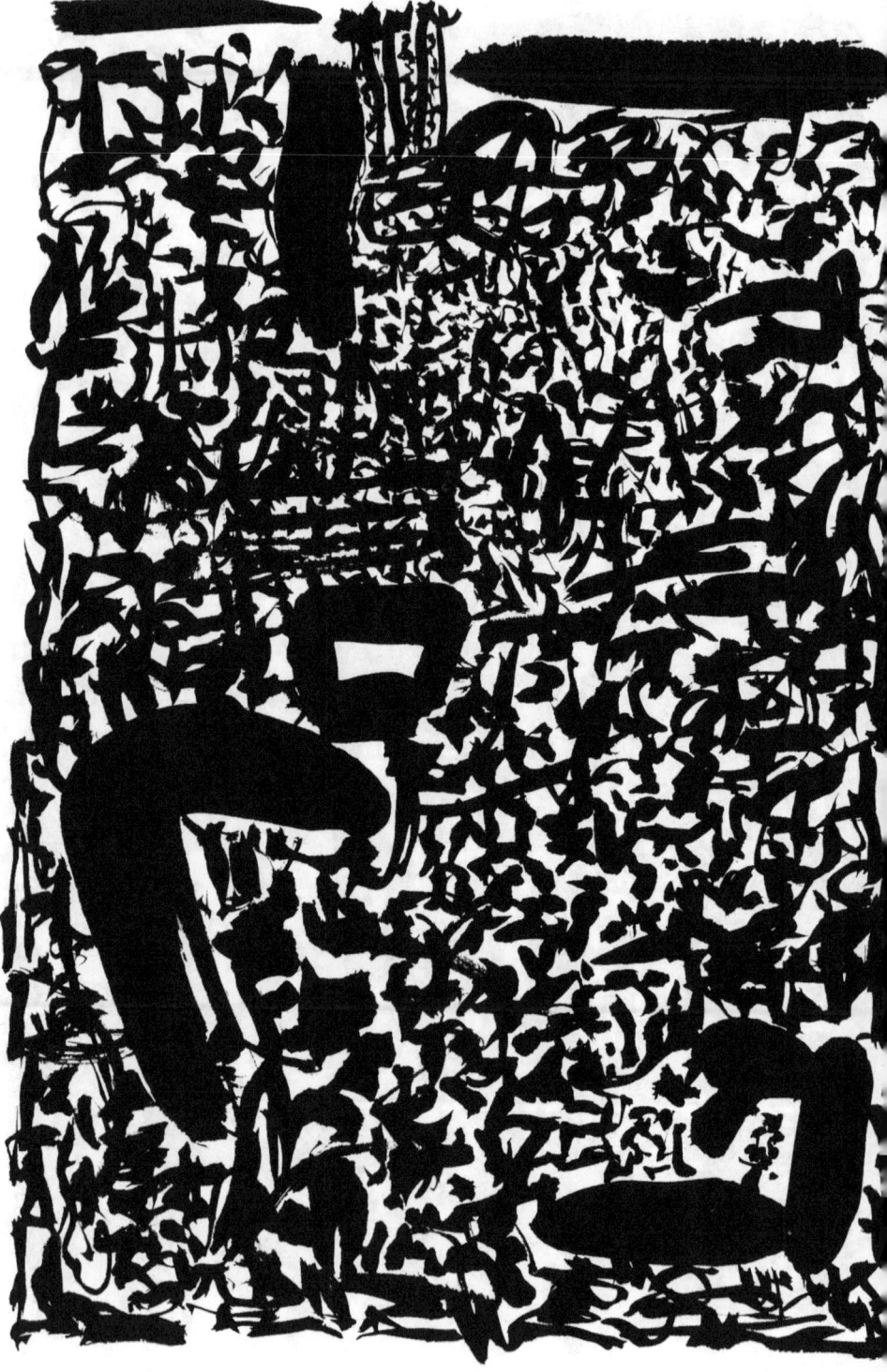

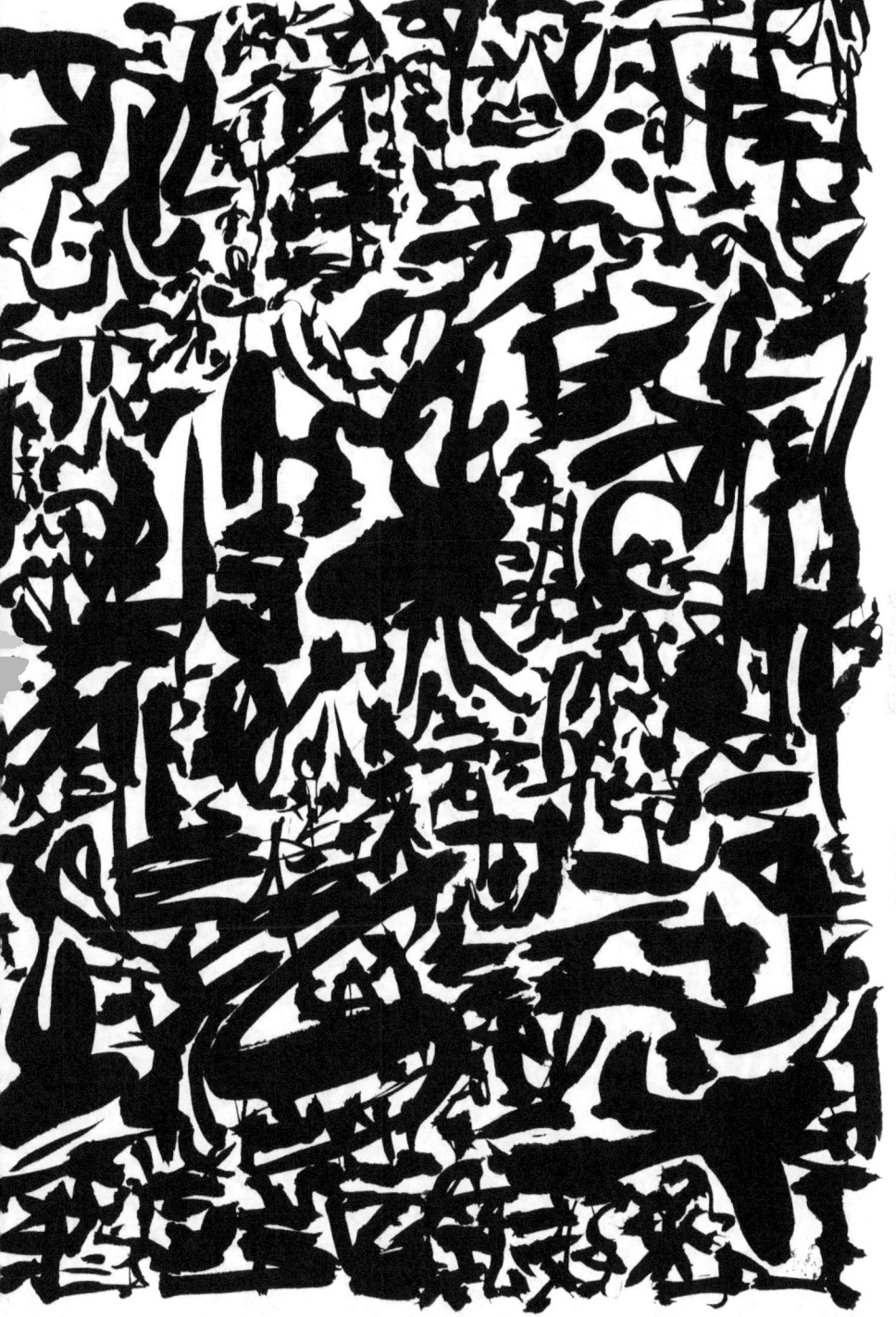

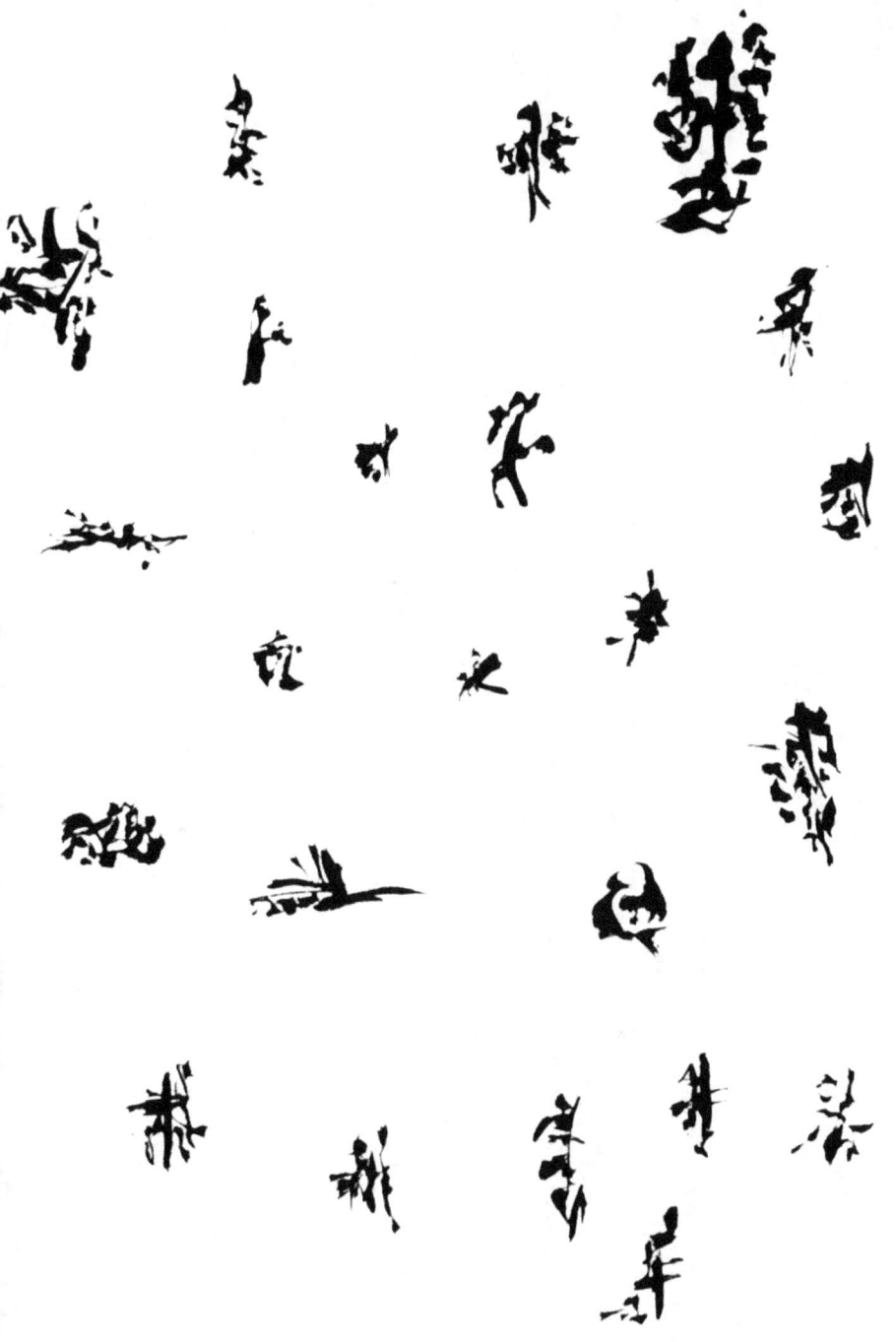

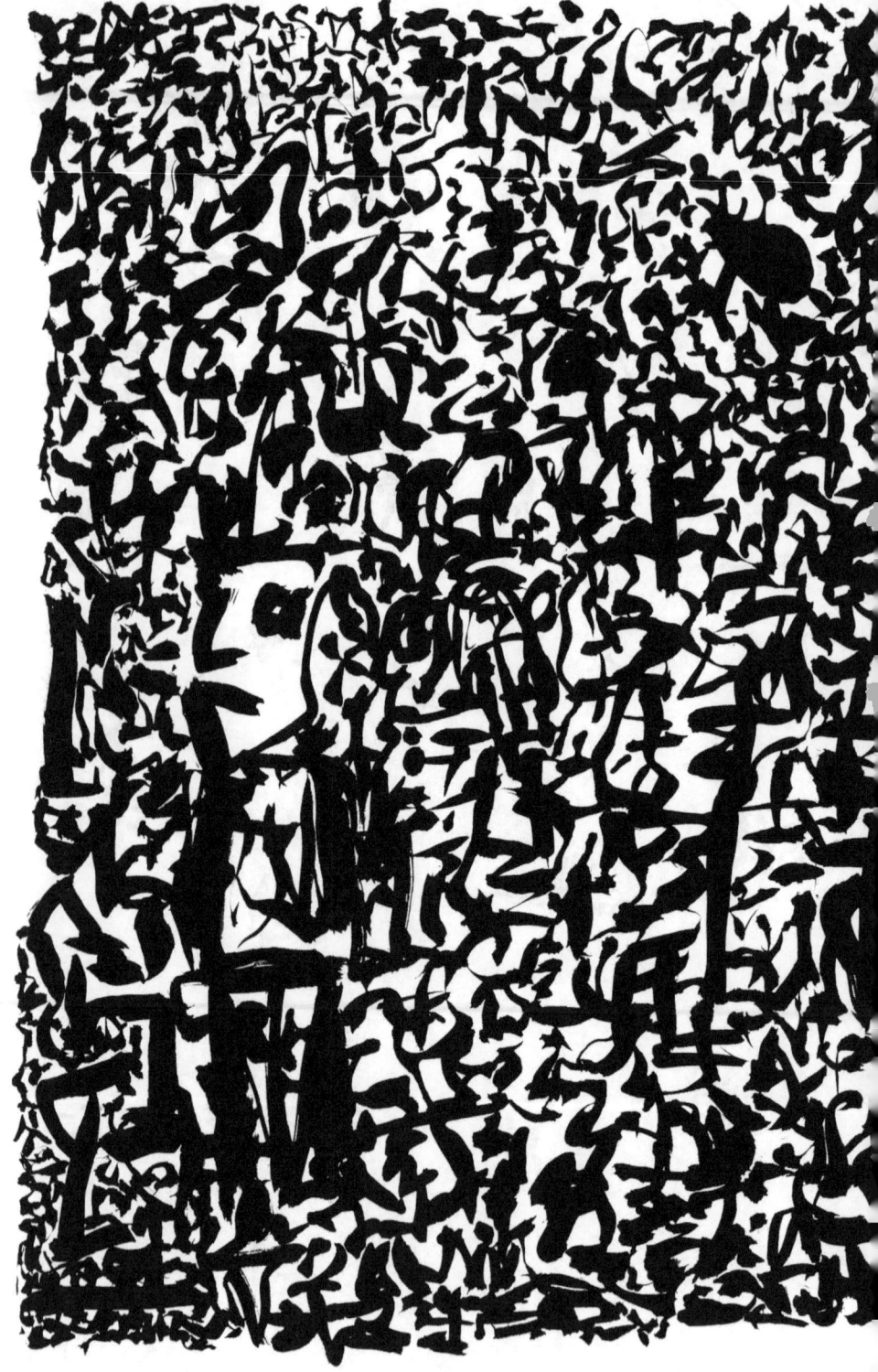

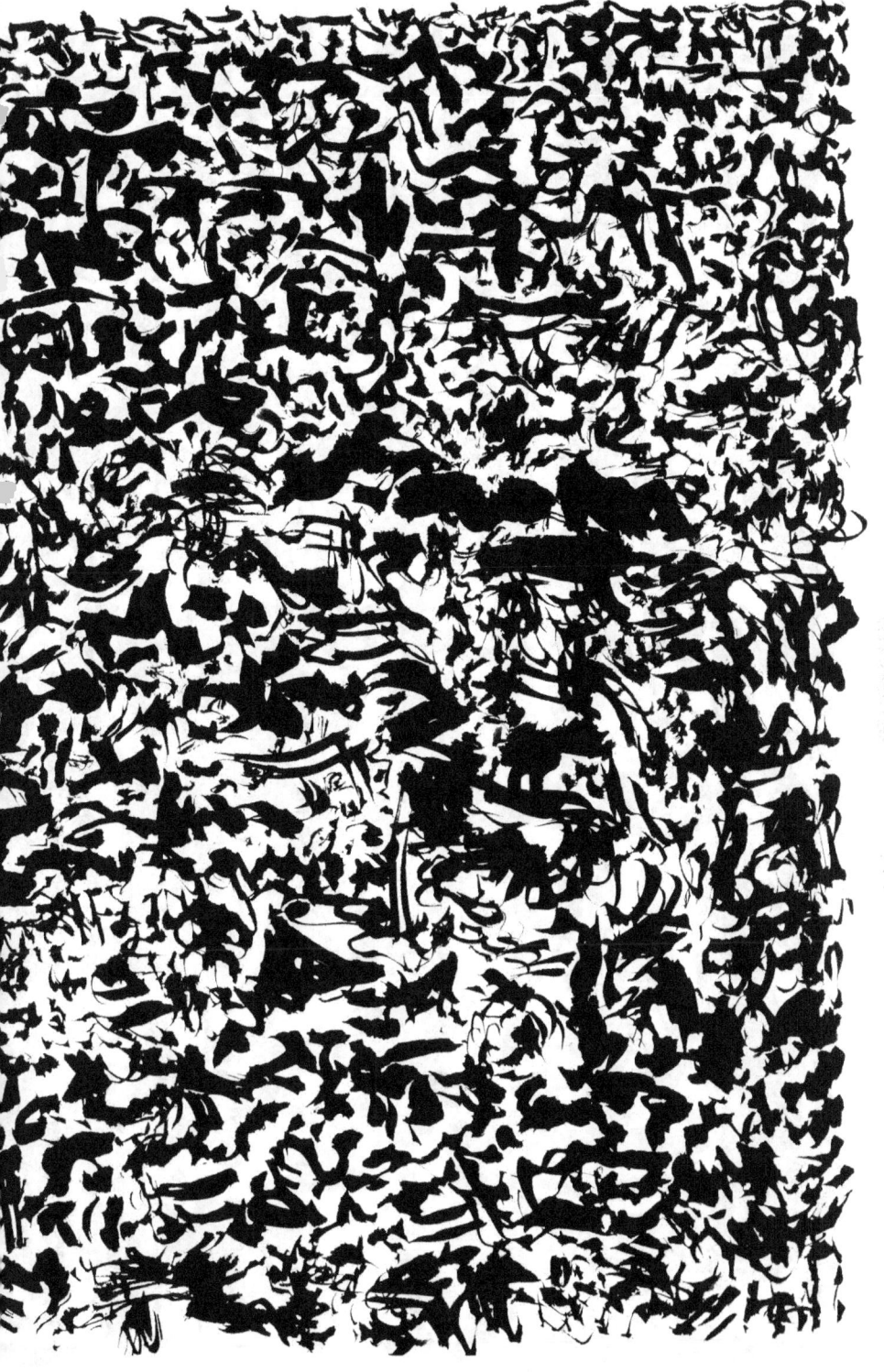

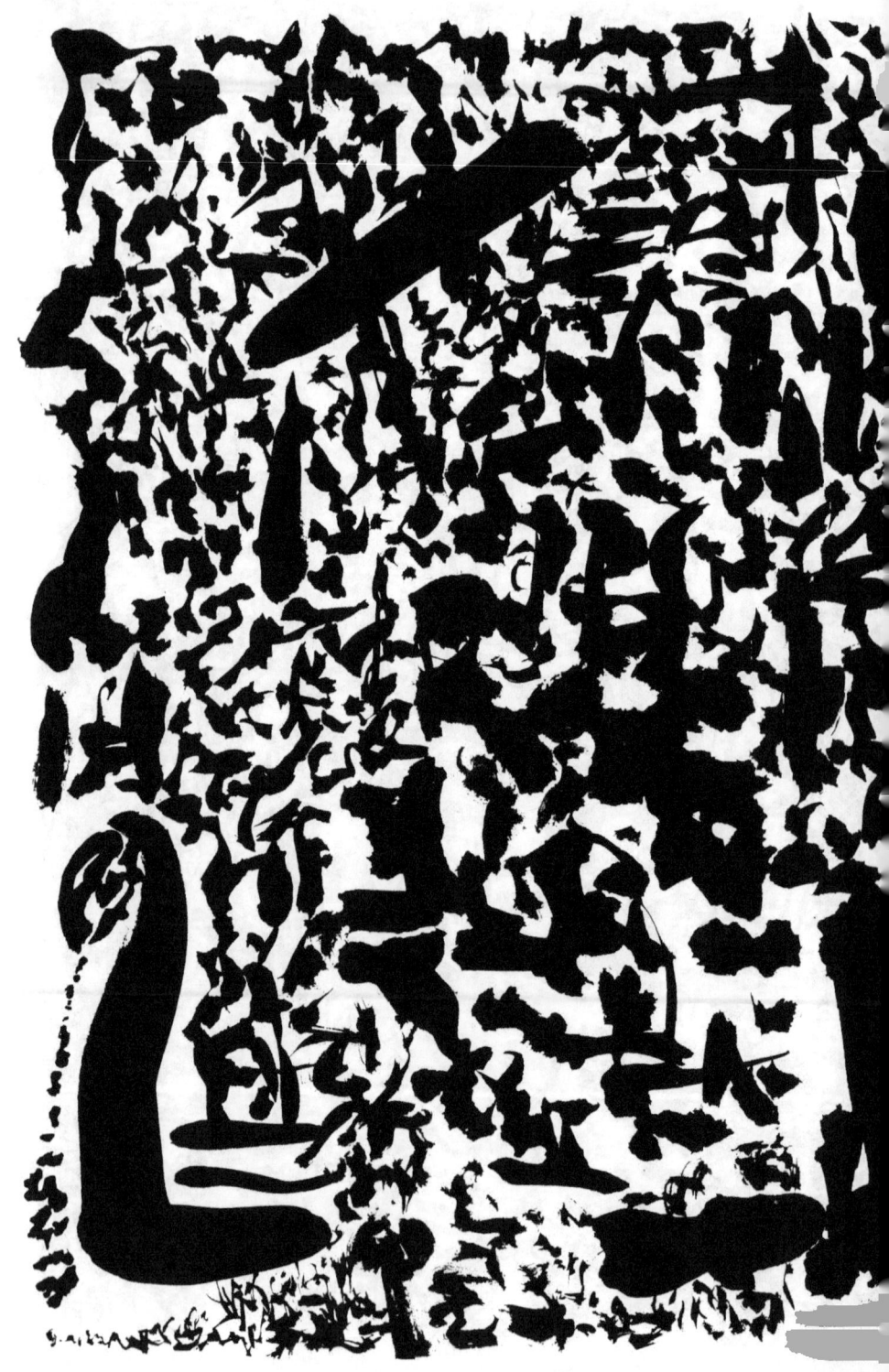

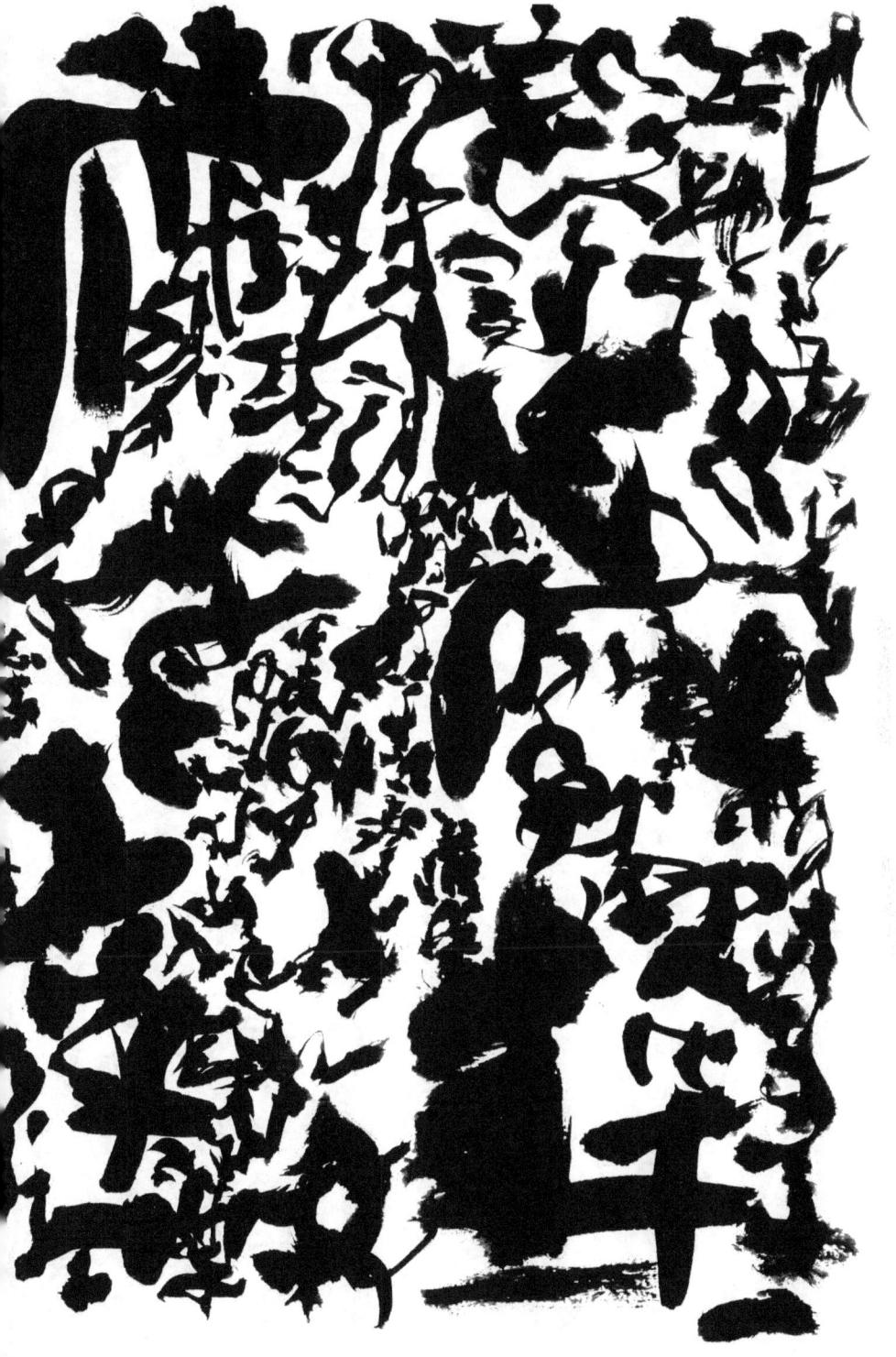

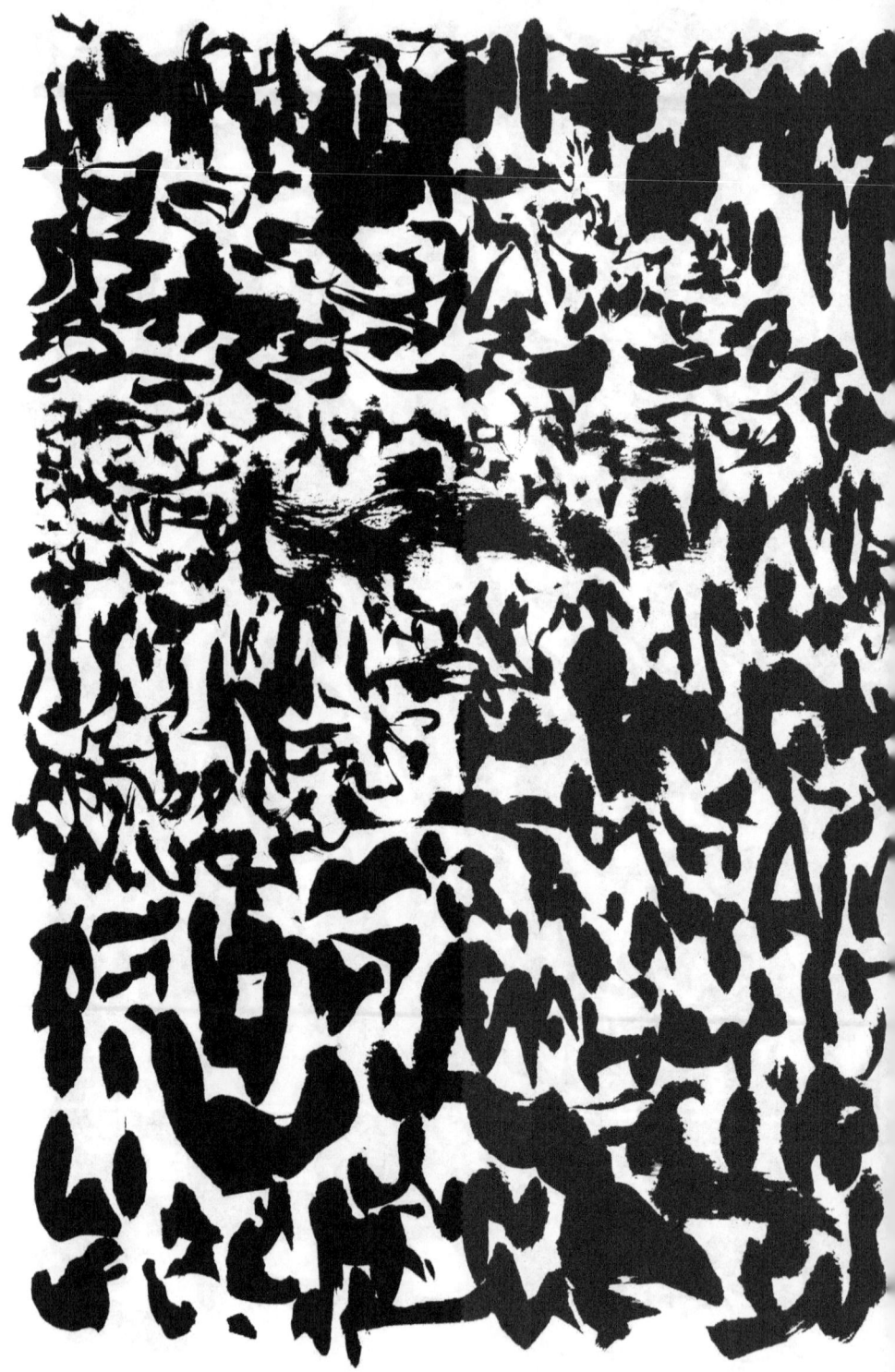

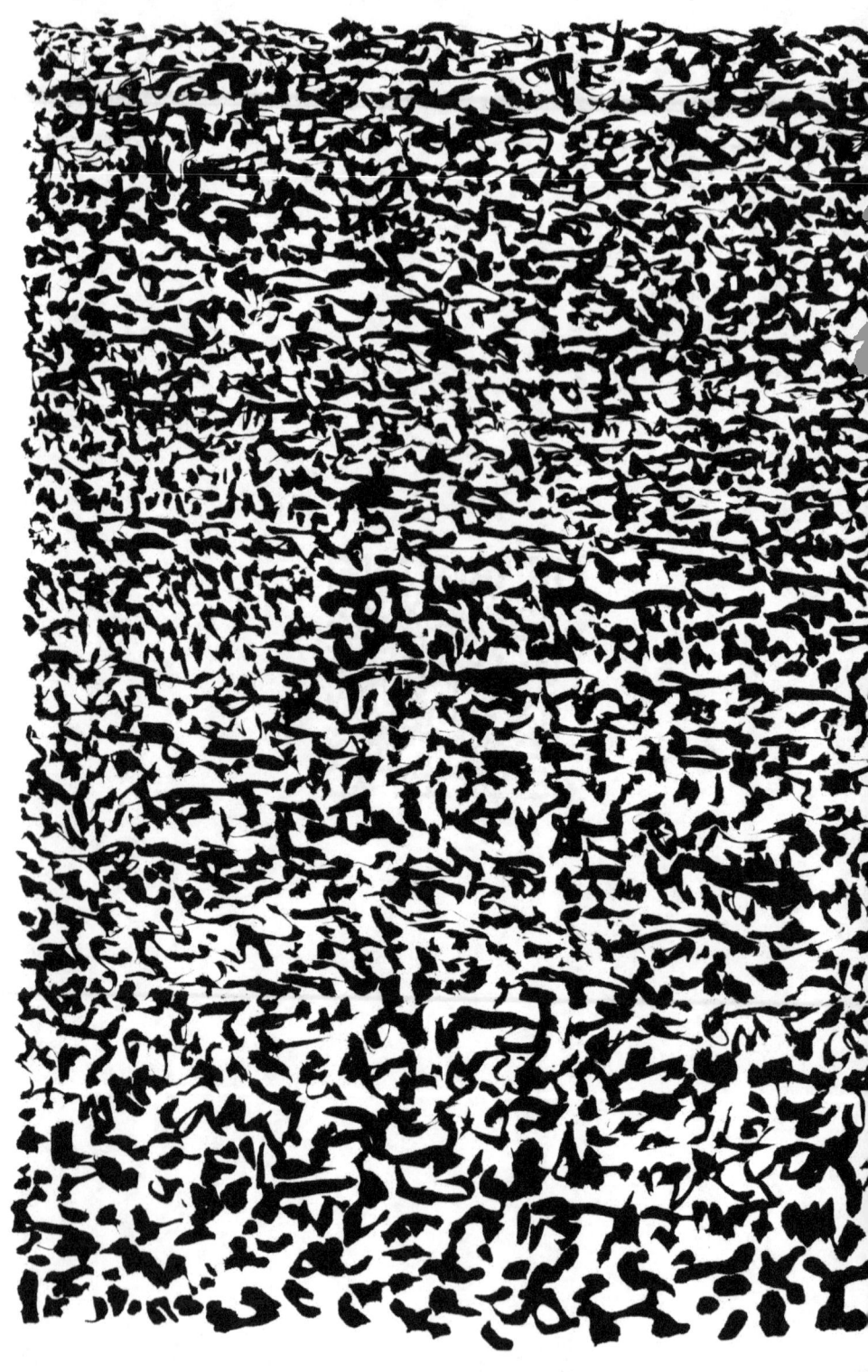

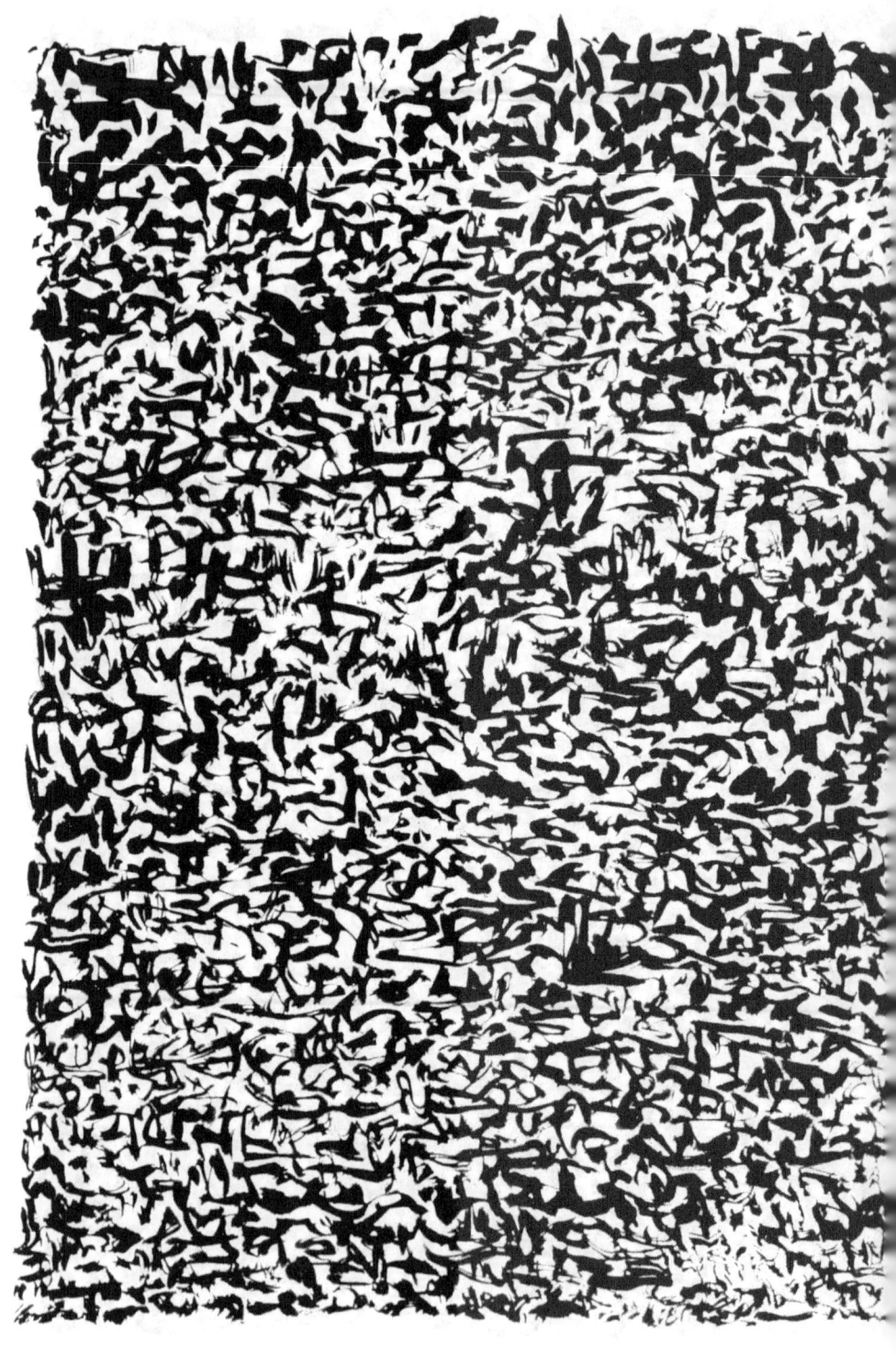

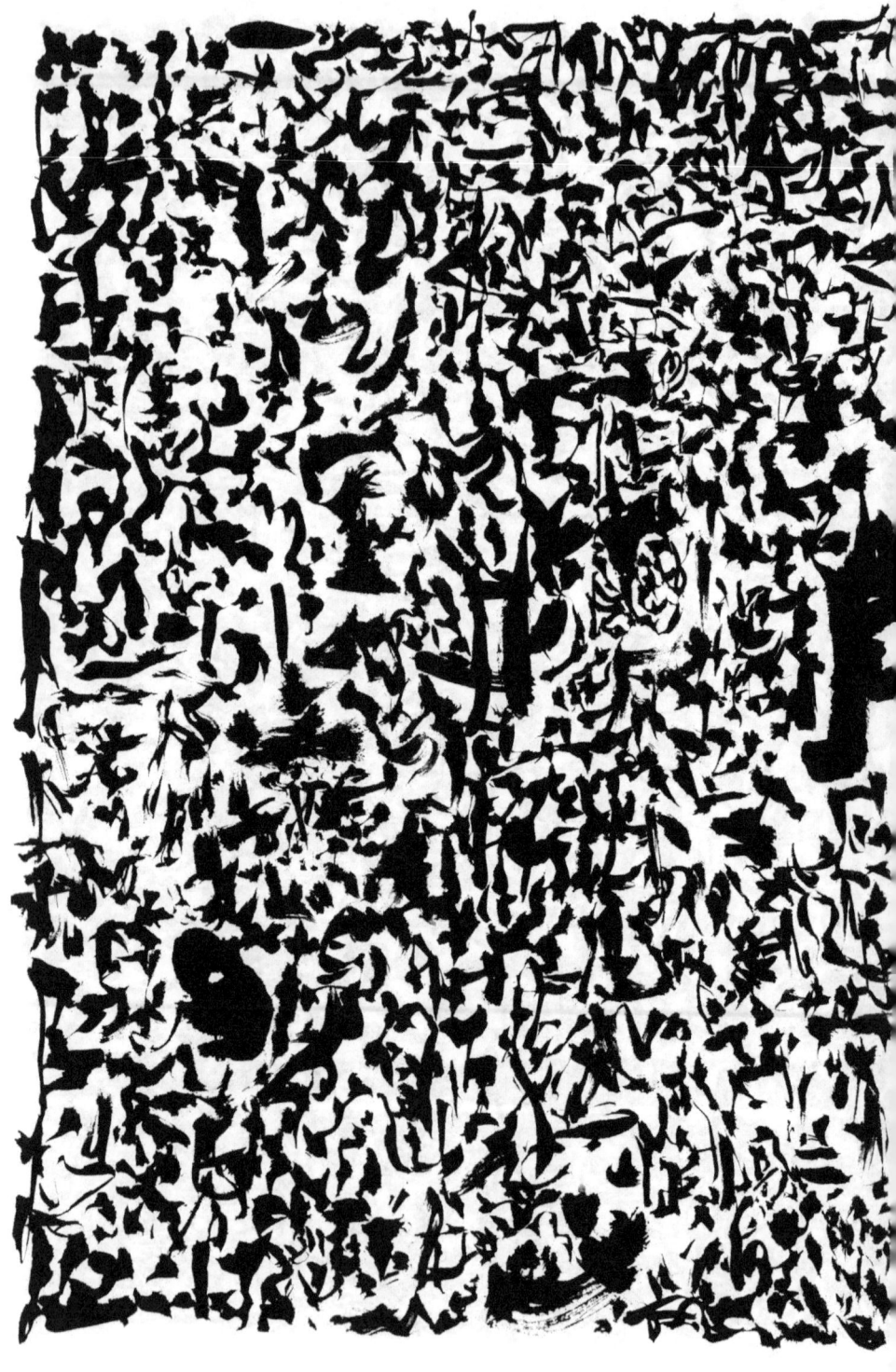

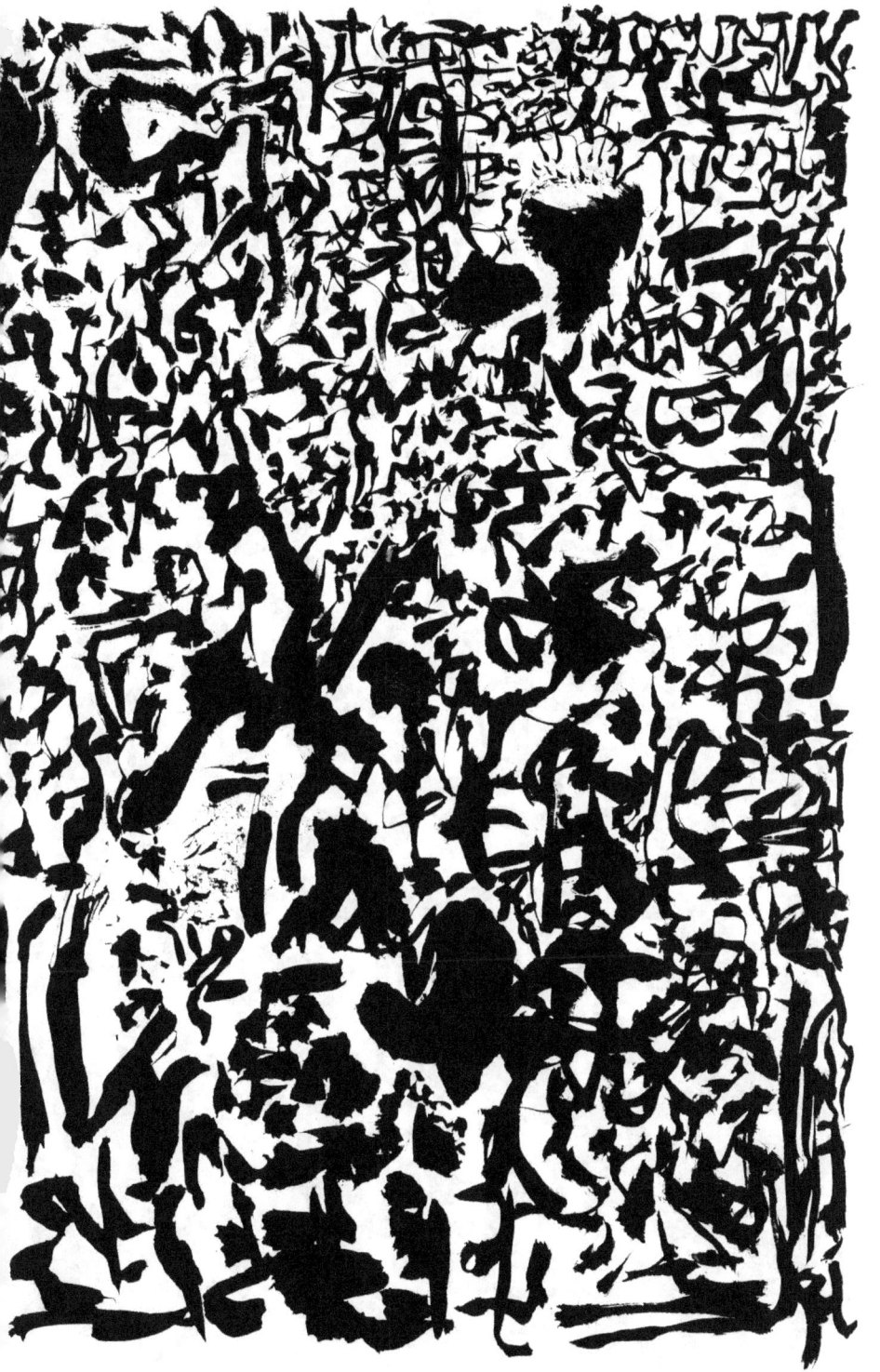

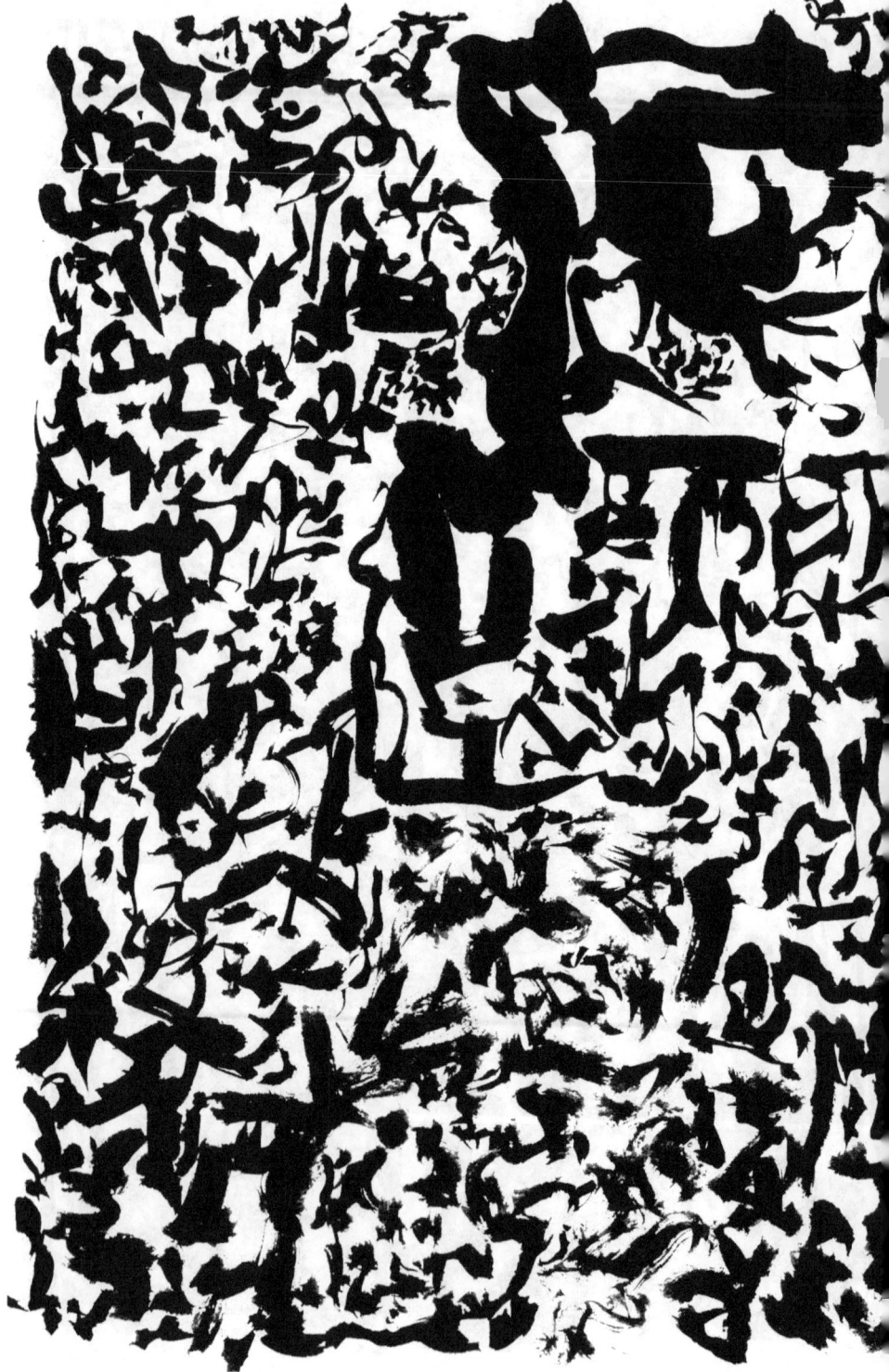

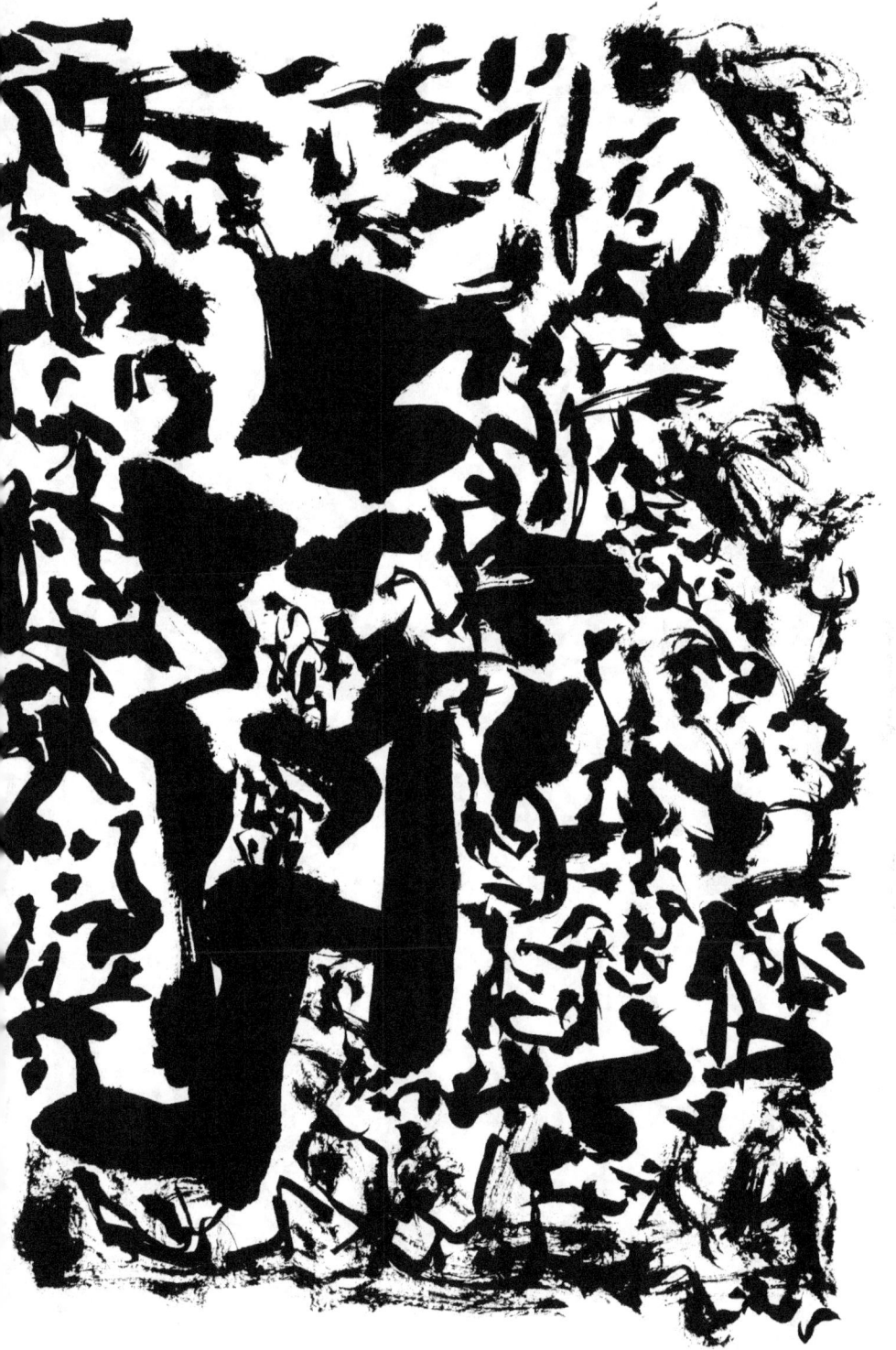

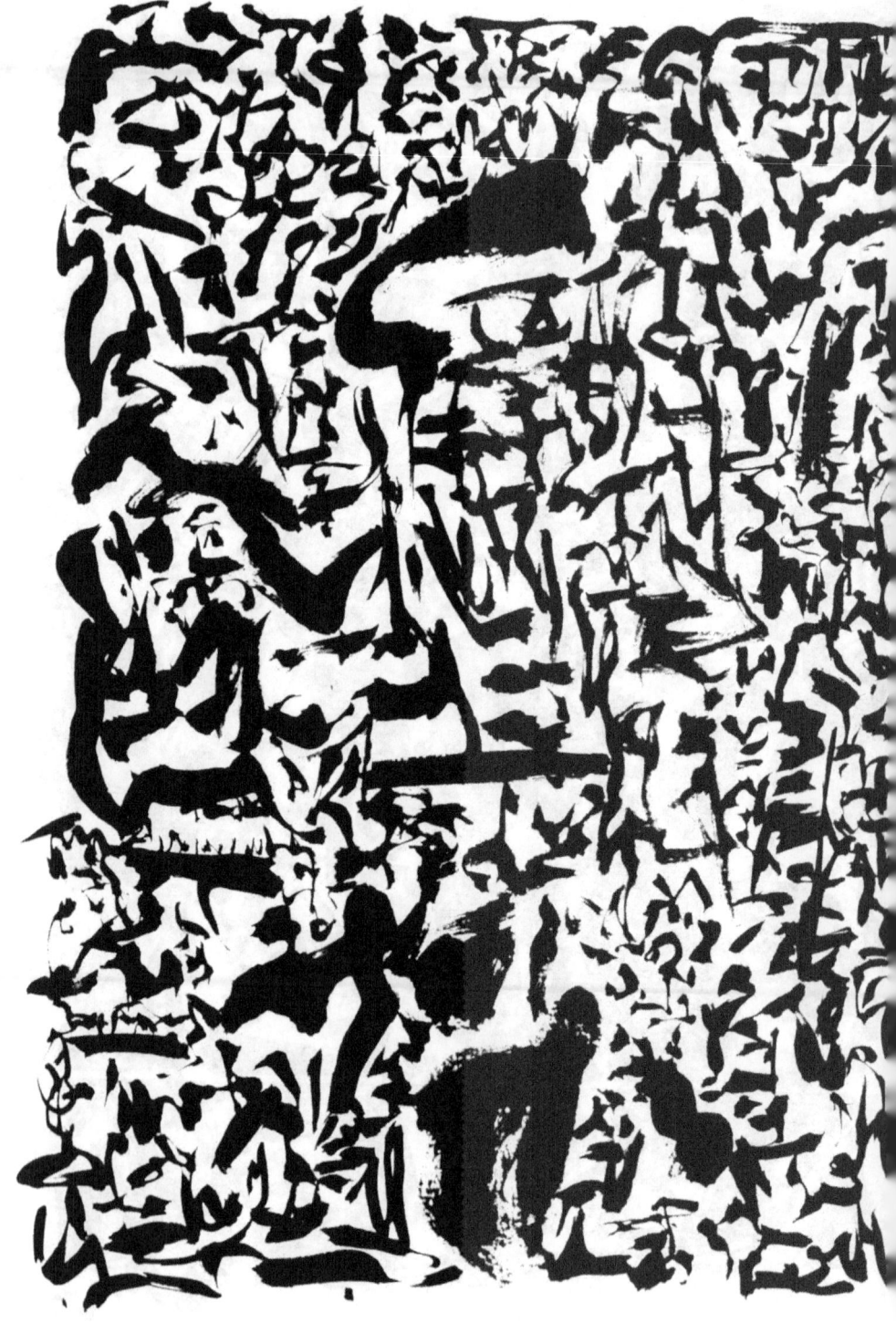

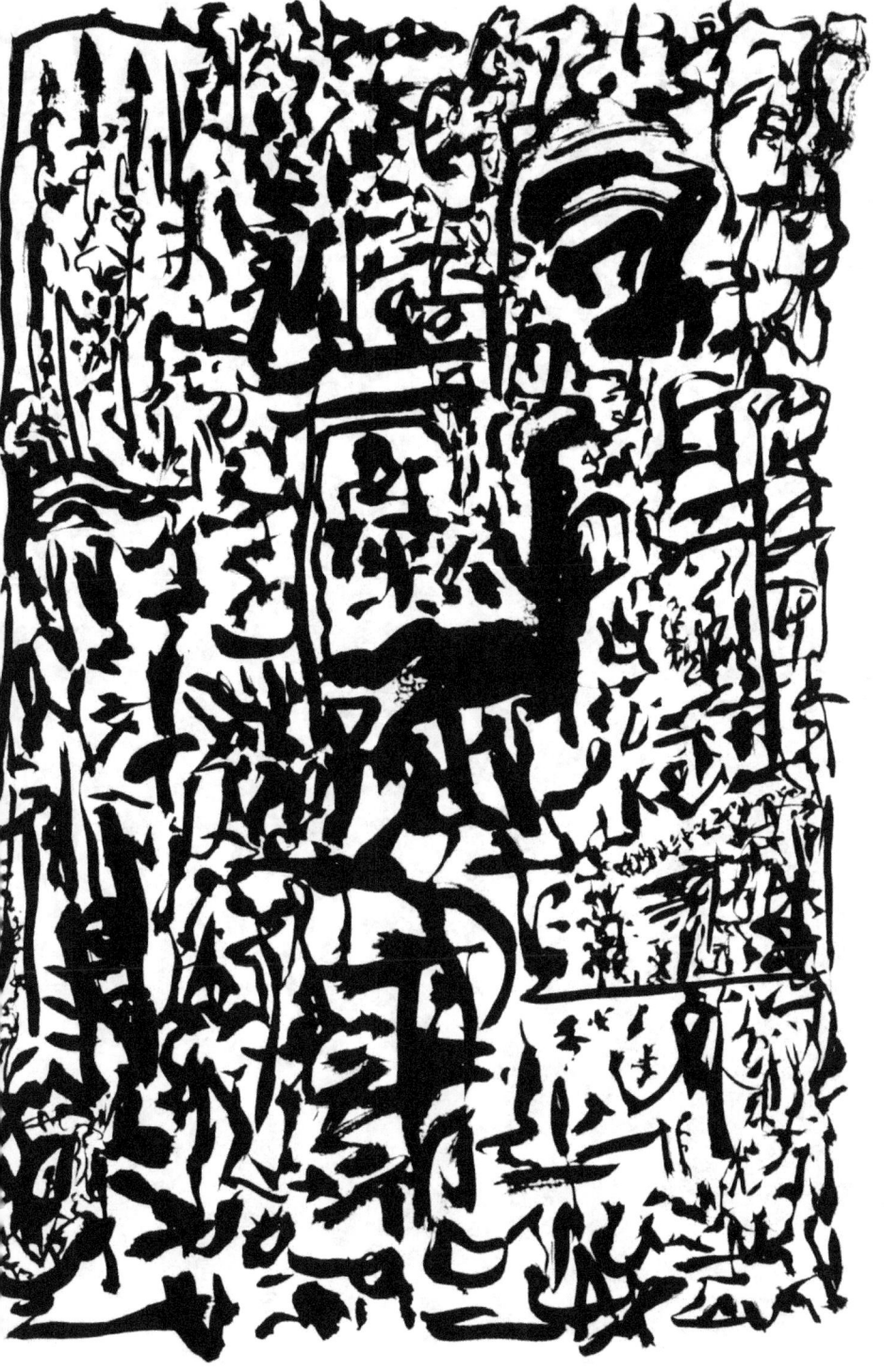

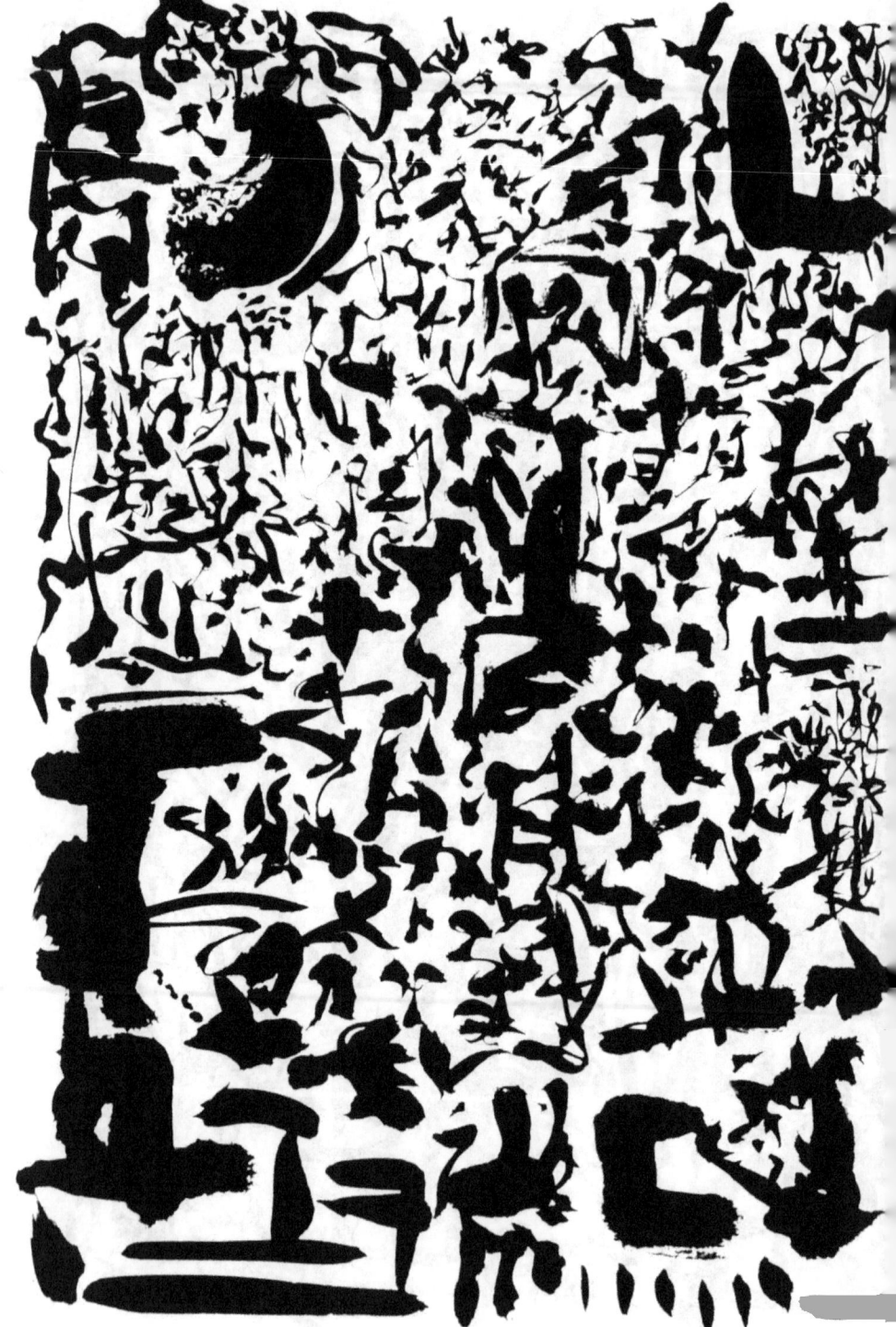

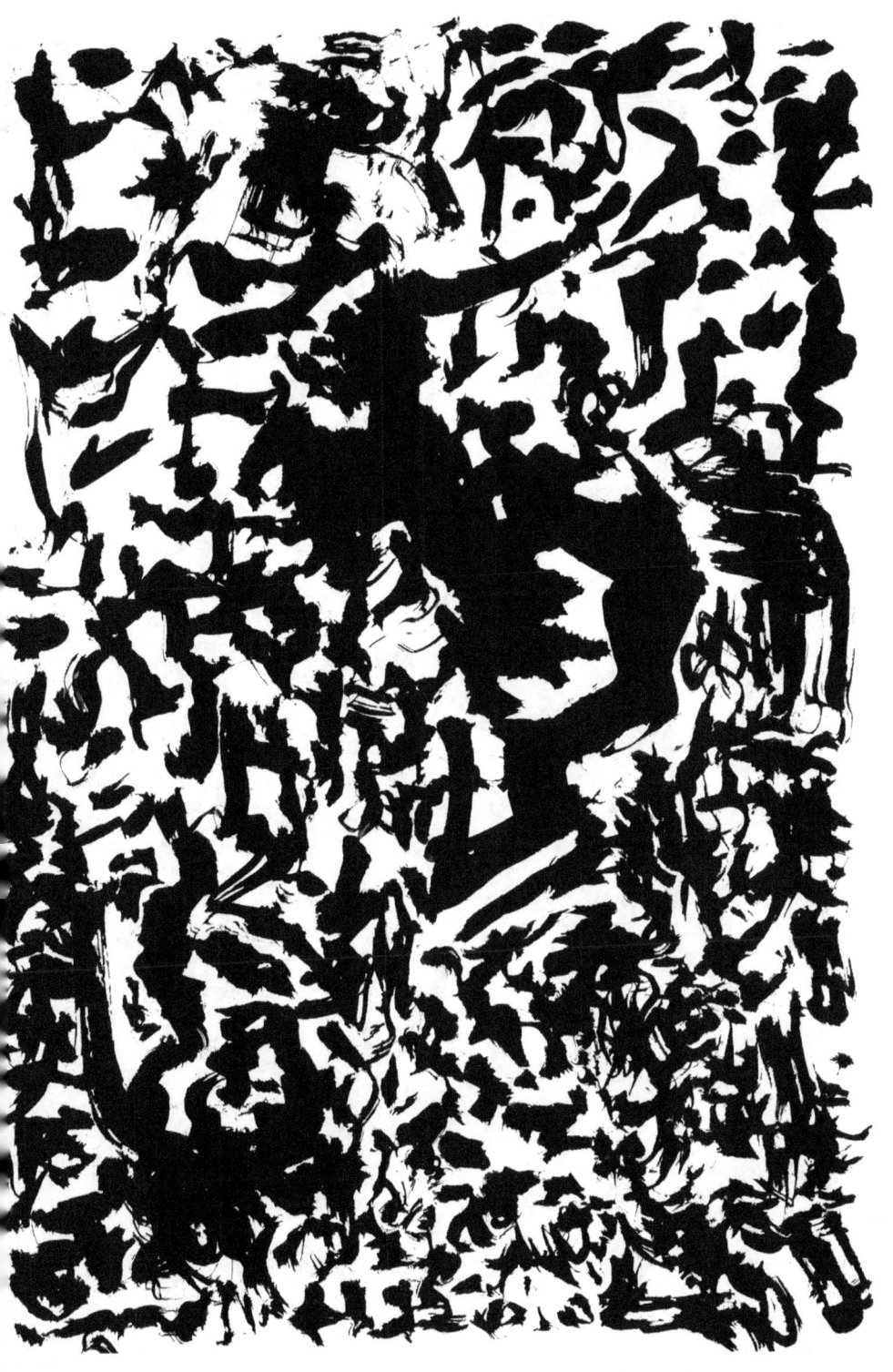

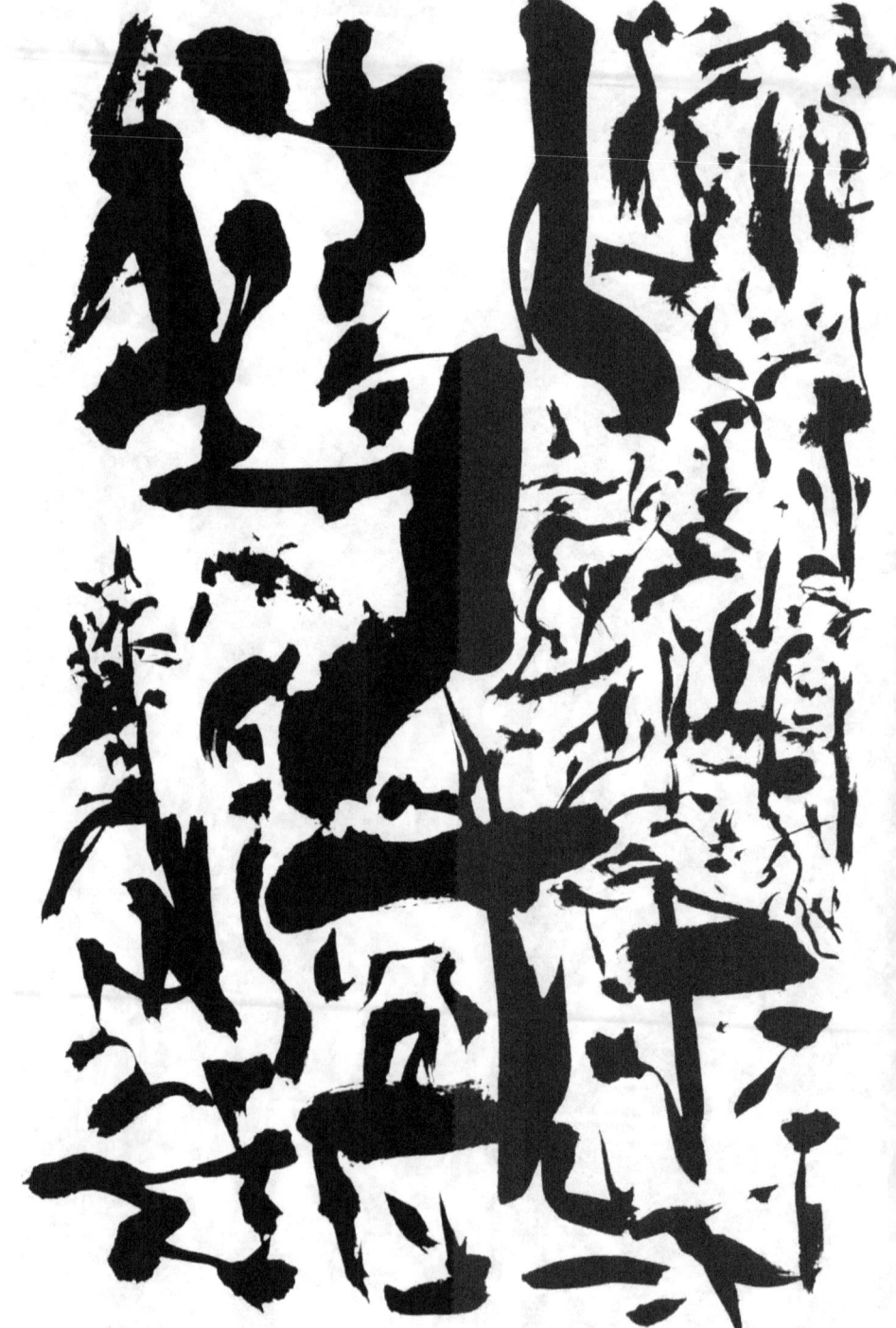

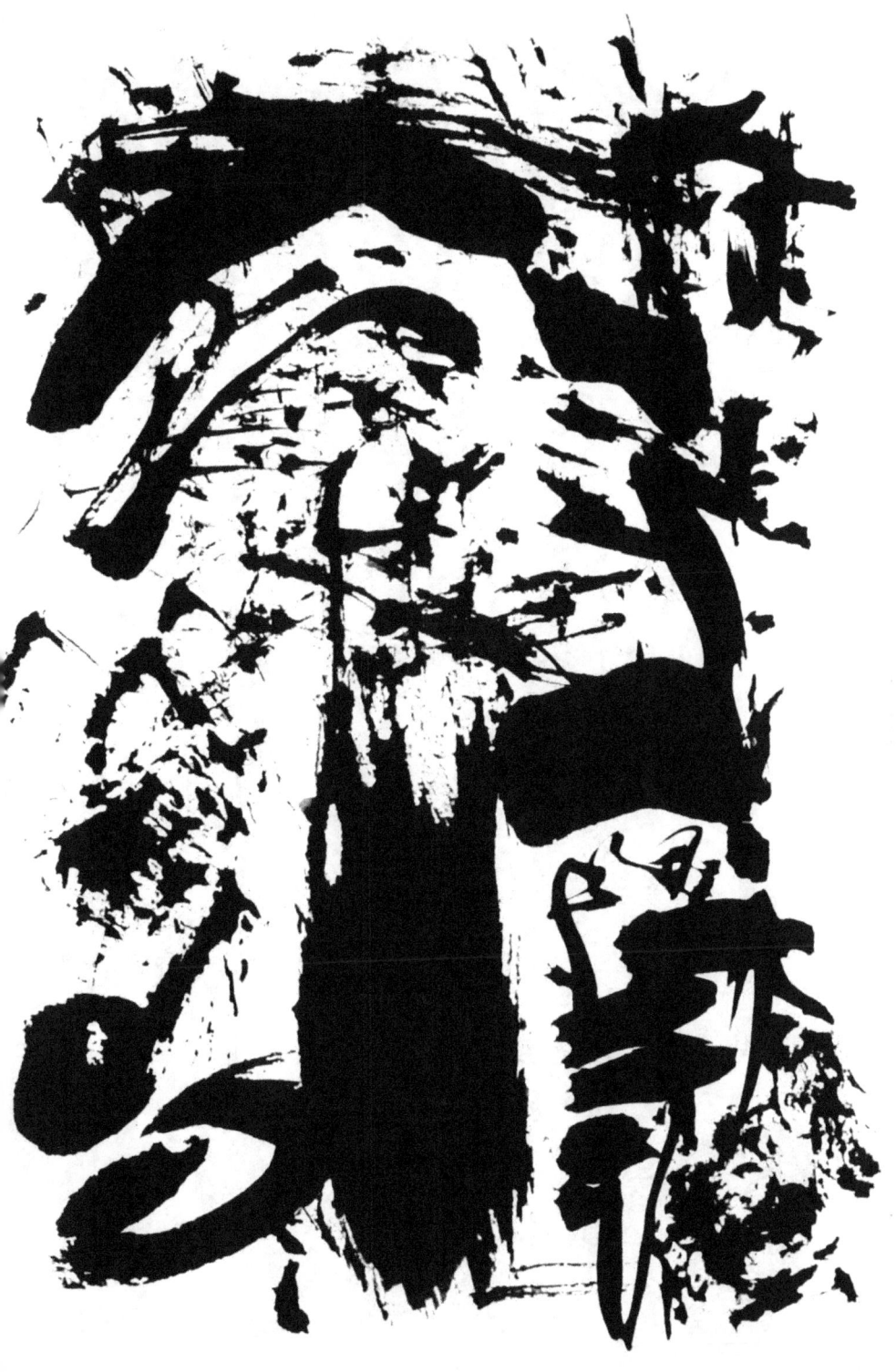

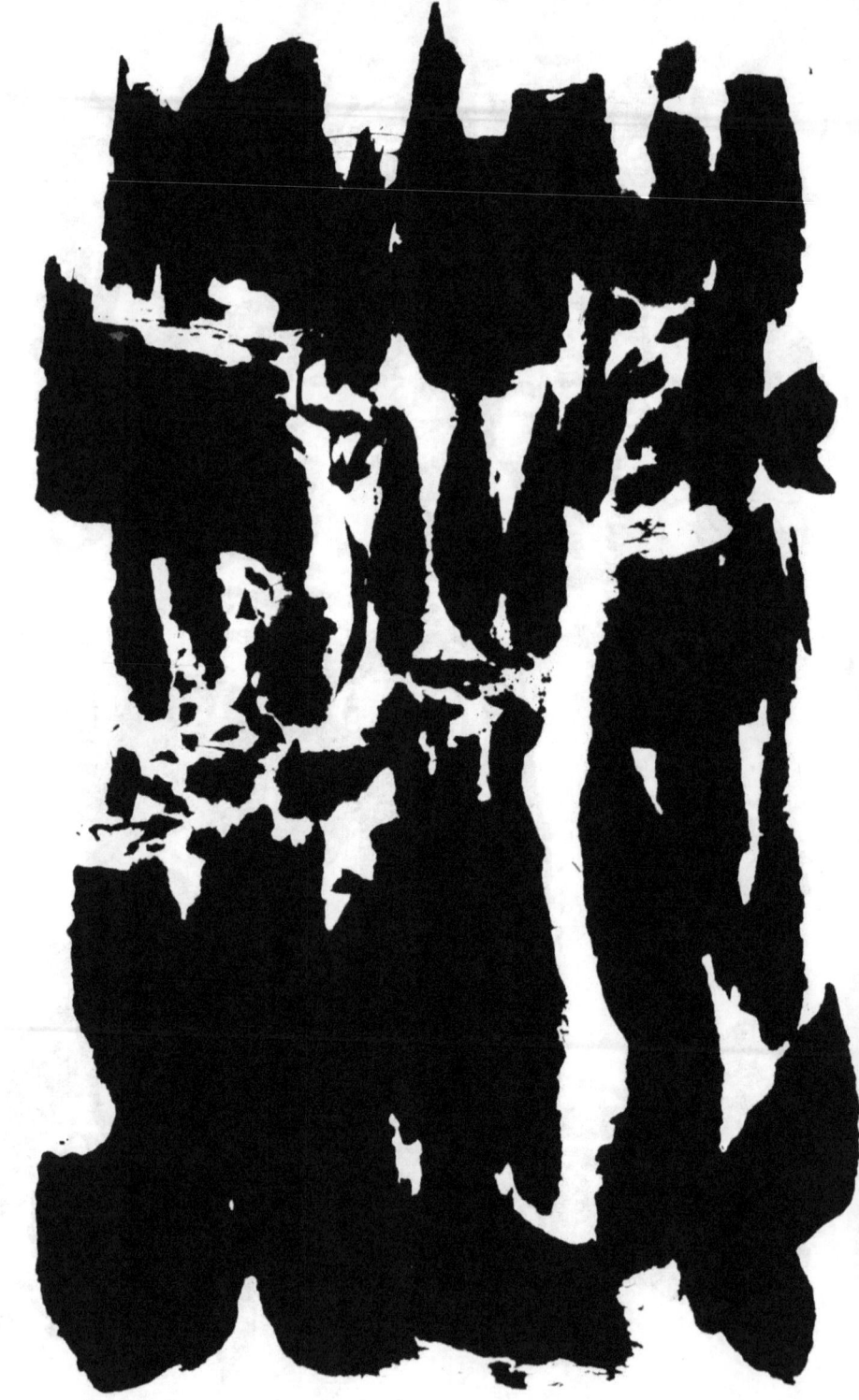

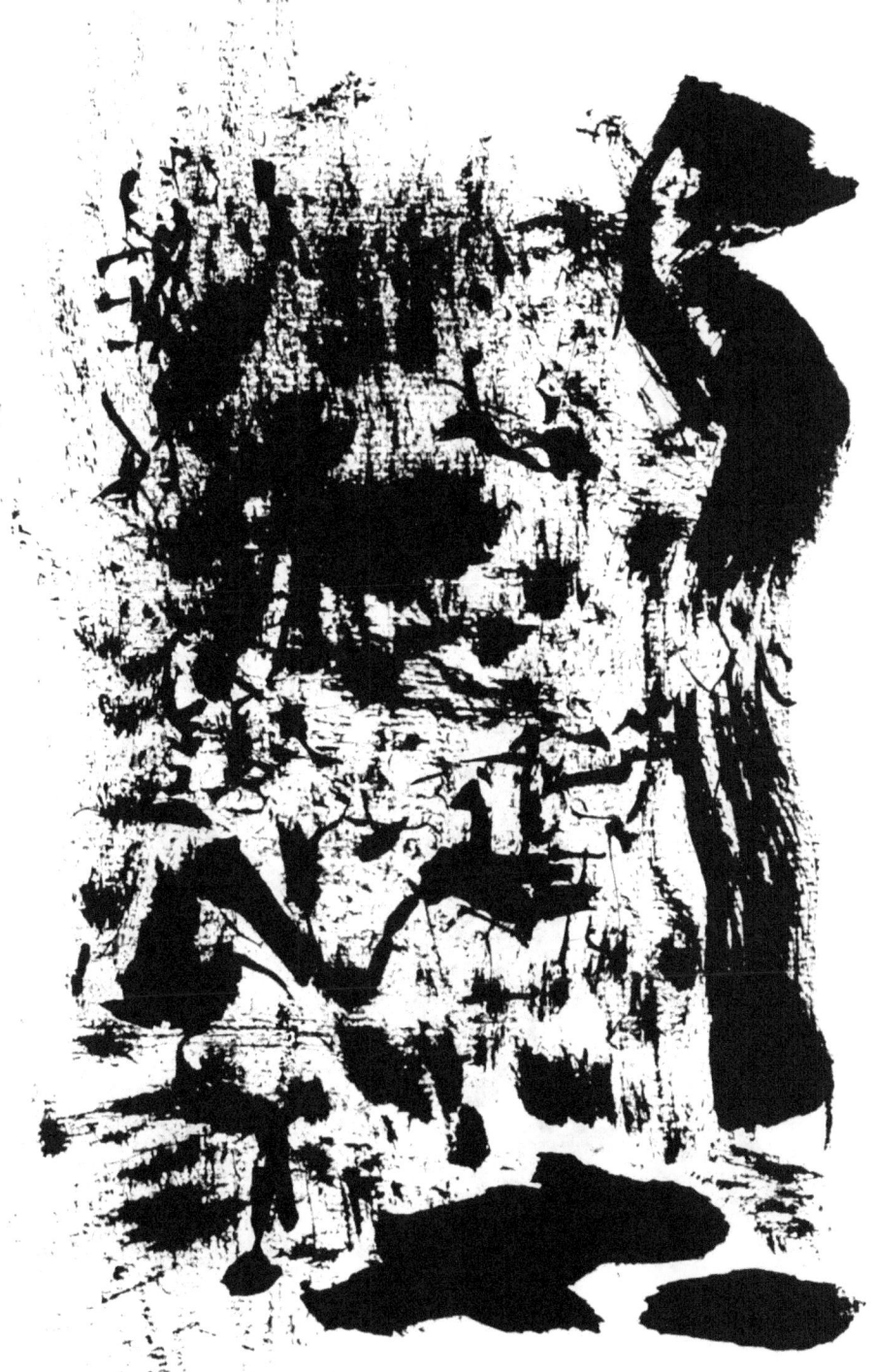

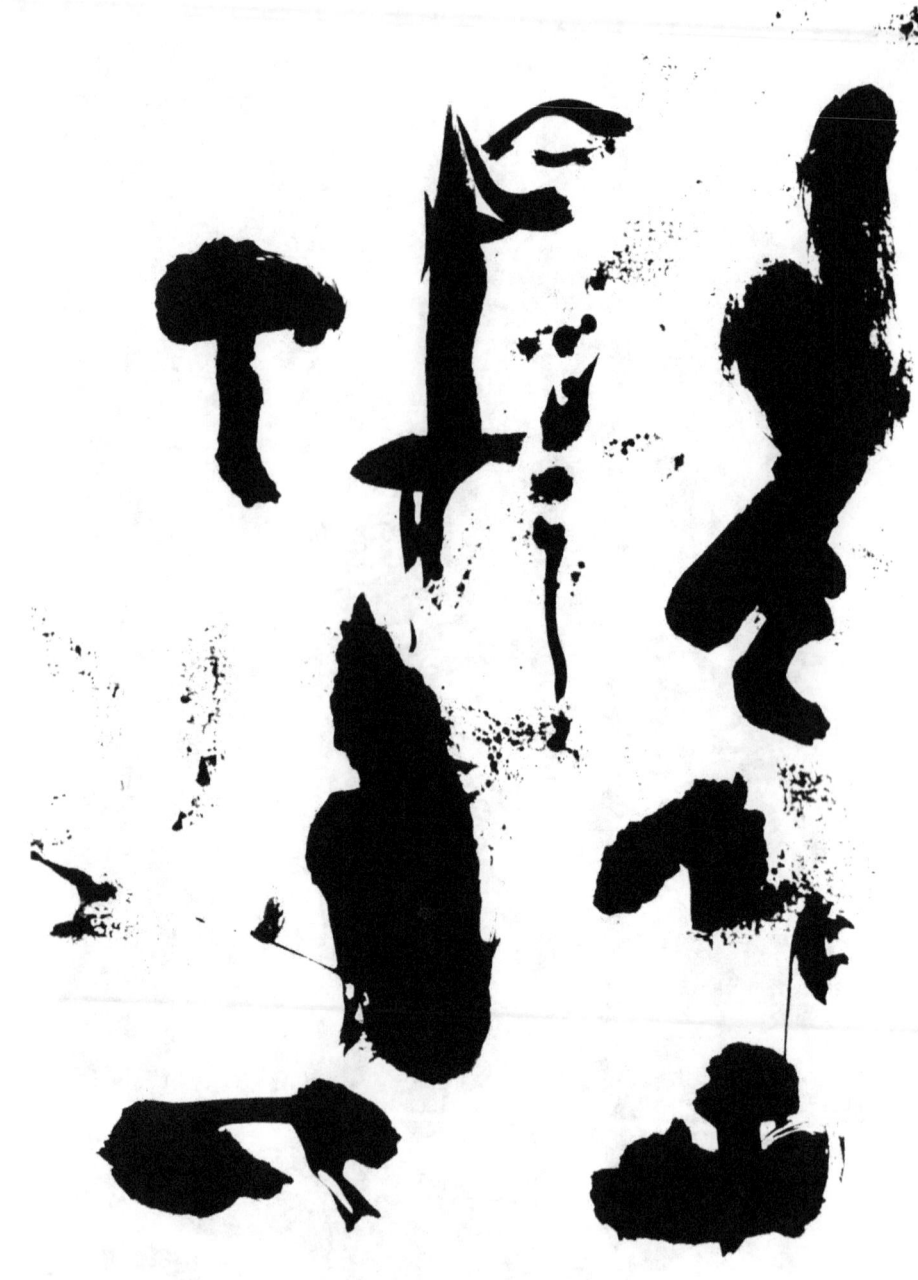

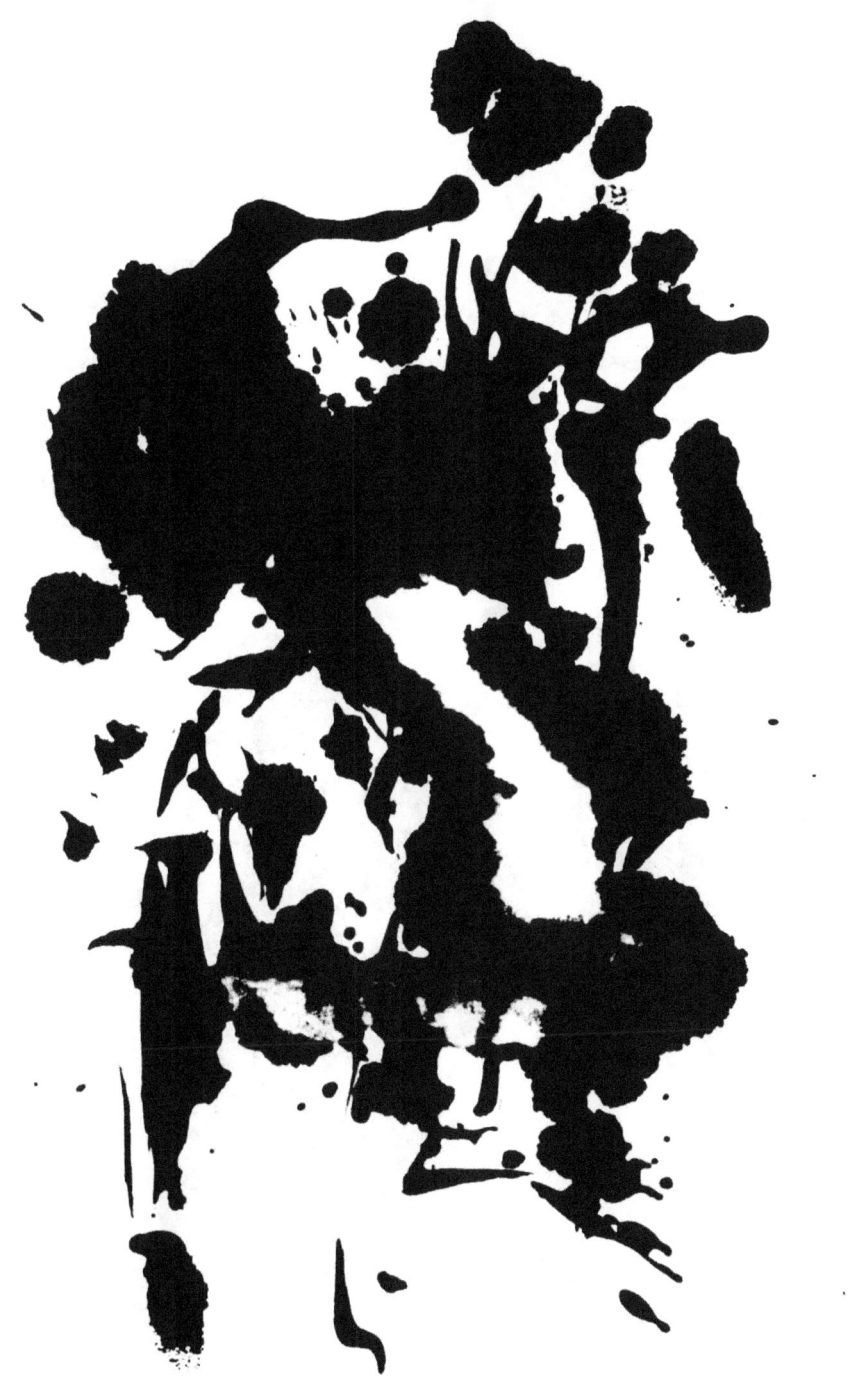

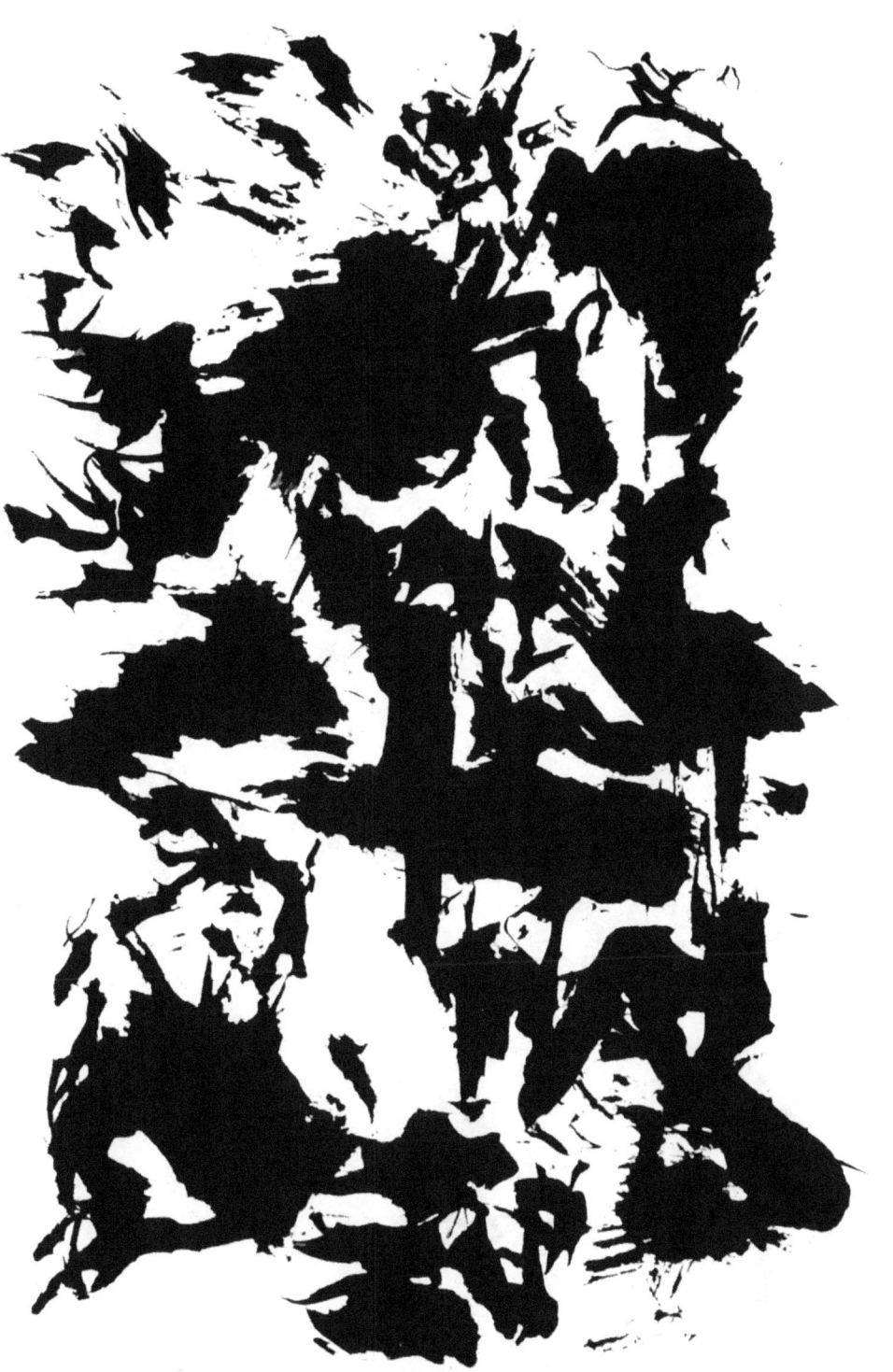

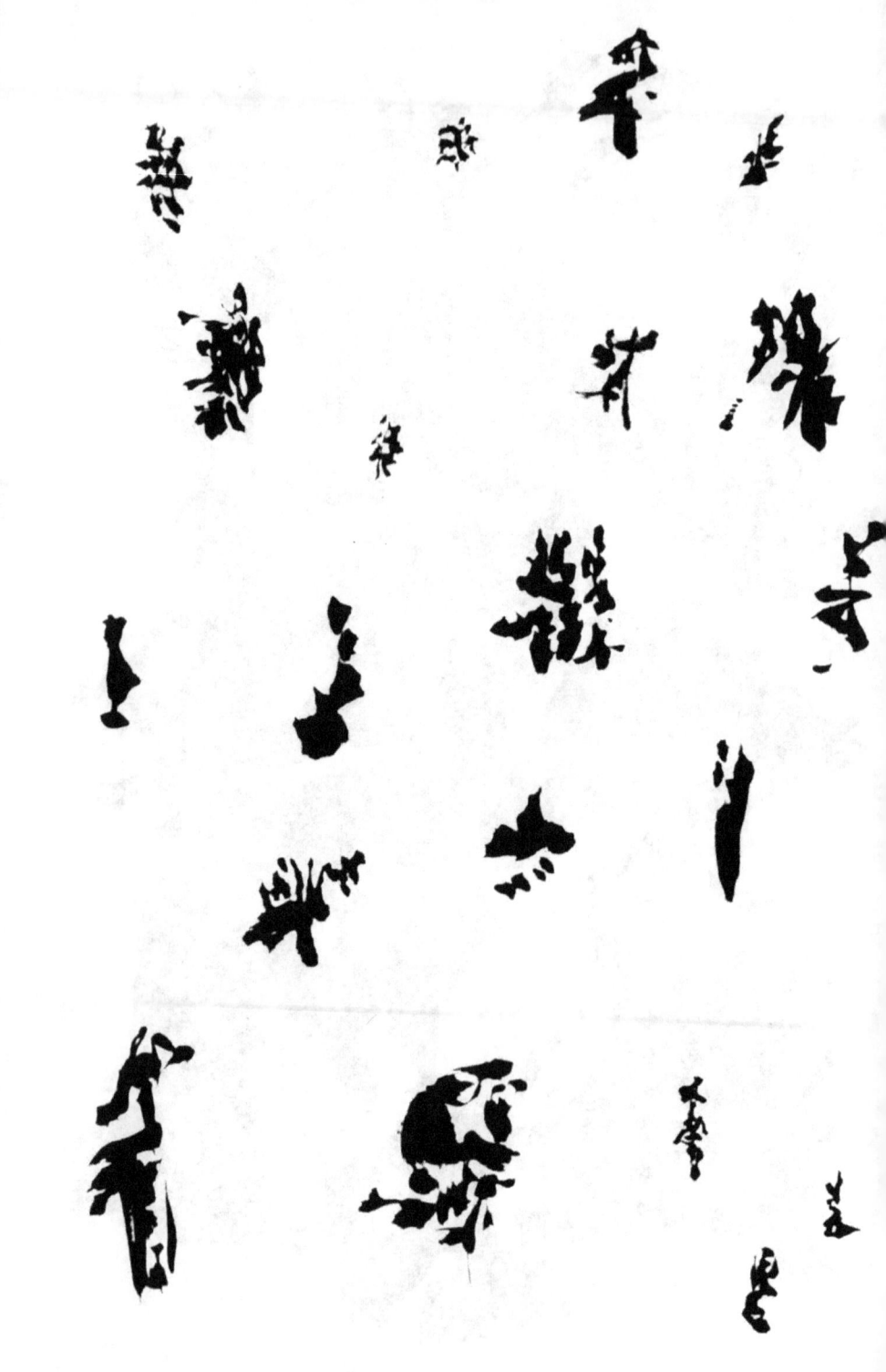

ASEMIC CONNOTATIONS
AND ASIA IN A BARBARIAN

SEANCORNELISSE